Integrated Reading

And Writing

Techniques, Essays, Arguments

Daniel V. Runyon, Ph.D.

Integrated Reading and Writing:

Techniques, Essays, Arguments

Daniel V. Runyon, Ph.D.

Copyright 2015 by Daniel V. Runyon

ISBN: 978 1 878559 23 4
Library of Congress Control Number: 2014920983
Saltbox Press
167 Burr Oak Drive
Spring Arbor, Michigan 49283

Price: $28.00

CONTENTS

INTRODUCTION

Integrating reading with writing is recognized as the new normal for learning to write at the college level, and the Dartmouth Institute for Writing and Rhetoric reports that it works best "when one process fuels or informs the other."

Teachers should limit the readings to brief examples so student have time to immediately write based on the sample. The best strategy is to "provide students with course readings that are well written, and take time in class to talk with students about what, exactly, makes the writing so good" (Dartmouth). Therefore, *Integrated Reading and Writing* offers a simple sequence for creating college papers:

1. Read the instructions and integrated reading provided
2. Respond thoughtfully to the analysis questions that follow each reading
3. Outline and write a first draft paper based on current knowledge
4. Add depth and credibility based on targeted research and literature reviews

5. If writing in Modern Language Association (MLA) format, consult the *MLA Handbook* cross-references provided. This text models MLA format. If writing in the American Psychological Association (APA) format, consult the Purdue Online Writing Lab (OWL) to correctly document sources https://owl.english.purdue.edu/owl/

6. Obtain peer reviewer guidance

7. Revise and polish the final draft

Following the strategy outlined above, *Integrated Reading and Writing* gives students the opportunity to explore their keen interests, control research, avoid plagiarism, and deliver their own arguments with power and persuasion.

The Strategy

Integrated Reading and Writing may be used in high school AP writing courses and accelerated home school settings as it is written at the 8.3 grade reading level. However, it is designed for composition courses at colleges and universities such as those represented by the CCCU[1] where courses are designed to integrate

---

[1] The Council for Christian Colleges & Universities (CCCU) has 120 members in North America and 58 affiliate institutions in 19 countries. The organization advances Christ-centered higher education and helps institutions transform

Christian faith with academic pursuits. Such schools promote the spiritual and intellectual development of servant-scholars with the ability to think and act critically as Christians across disciplinary boundaries.

This text accomplishes that vision by helping students encounter the Christian faith as they learn and apply the concepts of a Christian worldview, develop an ability to think creatively and critically, and demonstrate proficiency in research writing while expressing ideas logically.

The integrated approach recognizes that the best way to learn to write is to read and imitate good writing. Since third person is often required in formal writing, the concepts in each chapter are explained in third person. Since instructions are usually given in second person, the text uses second person with the analysis questions, writing assignments, and peer review guidelines. The text deliberately shows students how to do everything expected of them.

Each chapter contains readings that model the type of writing under investigation so students first have a style of writing explained, then have that form of writing

---

lives by faithfully relating scholarship and service to biblical truth.

9

modeled, followed by assignments giving them opportunity to write in the same vein. Analysis questions after each reading are targeted to achieve Bloom's Taxonomy objectives of evaluation, synthesis, analysis, application, understanding, and knowledge (Dalton). Responding to the questions both aids students in comprehension and trains them to ask the kinds of questions useful when doing textual analysis.

Peer review exercises specific to each chapter function as a form of test marketing as students practice the art of connecting with their audience while engaging interactively in the writing process, which usually requires extensive editing and rewriting. Peer reviews also give students opportunity to teach others, an educational strategy recognizing that one effective way to learn a thing is to teach it.

Integrated Reading and Writing builds from simple to more complex forms of writing—from techniques to essays to arguments—while teaching research skills in a progressive fashion so students are not overwhelmed by the complexity of MLA or APA documentation. Few attempts are made to give instruction on the fundamentals of grammar and punctuation since that is ably covered in the *MLA Stylebook,* and cross-references to that book are included.

The Foundation

"Before time itself was measured, the Voice was speaking" (John 1:1). The Voice is the *logos*, the root of the English word "logic." A better source demonstrating how to think, and how to find a voice, will never exist. Using biblical passages to model effective writing makes sense from the practical standpoint because the Bible is the most widely read and continuously published book in the history of humankind. David Van Biema writes in *Time* magazine, "Not only is the Bible the best-selling book of all time, it is the best-selling book of the year every year," and students "need the Bible to make sense of the ideas and rhetoric that have helped drive U.S. history" (43).

T. R. Henn says the Bible provides the Western tradition with its "single greatest source" (258). Northrop Frye calls the Bible "the major informing influence on literary symbolism" (*Anatomy of Criticism* 316).[2] The symbols and images used in the Bible pervade western literature. Frye's list includes city, mountain, river,

---

[2] See also Leland Ryken, *The Literature of the Bible* (Grand Rapids: Zondervan, 1974), and Rene Wellek and Austin Warren, "The Nature of Literature," *Theory of Literature*, 3rd ed. (New York: Harcourt, Brace and World, 1956) 20-28.

11

garden, tree, oil, fountain, bread, wine, bride, and sheep. These images "indicate some kind of unifying principle," and Frye identifies "a unified structure of narrative and imagery in the Bible" (*The Great Code: The Bible and Literature* xiii).[3] These critics are contending that knowledge of the Bible is essential to comprehending *any* western literature.

Students need knowledge of the Bible both for its content and for its presentation of that content, as Mark Twain explains: "It is hard to make a choice of the most beautiful passage in a book which is so gemmed with beautiful passages as the Bible.... Who taught those ancient writers their simplicity of language, their felicity of expression, their pathos, and above all, their faculty of sinking themselves entirely out of sight of the reader and making the narrative stand out alone and seem to tell itself?" (*The Innocents Abroad* 220).

The Bible is foundational for students interested in the art of literary criticism, and it is an effective tool for teaching writers in every discipline how to communicate both simple and complex thoughts. In addition to its interesting stories and great poetry, the Bible also

---

[3] Frye's "Great Code" language comes from Blake, who said, "The Old and New Testaments are the Great Code of Art" (quoted in Frye xvi).

contains timeless truth. Reading and thinking about the masterpieces modeled therein helps students become better people as well as better writers and thinkers.

The Assignments

All the major readings in this text are accompanied by analysis questions that help students imprint what they have read into their memories by carrying on a written conversation with the author. Students should imagine the author as a personal friend talking directly to them over a delicious beverage. They can ask the author questions, thank him for wise advice, complain about what he has not said that they wish they knew, or mention related information they already know.

Student responses to the analysis questions demonstrate the ability to "think" on paper by responding quickly, yet sensibly, to ideas. Also, good writing is the result of continual rewriting, and student responses to analysis questions represent first thoughts and ideas that may develop into carefully crafted research papers. Just as art students look at models as they draw or paint, so writing students following the models provided in *Integrated Reading and Writing* will write something that resembles what they have just read. It makes sense that students would read a chapter about narrative writing, respond in writing to a sample narrative, and then write their own narrative. Students are invited to imitate—but not plagiarize—sample writings.[4]

Following the strategies outlined in this text helps teachers hold in check the proliferation of electronic file sharing and plagiarism common in the educational system today. Students must show the developmental path of their writing through their answers to analysis questions, their first draft of the actual writing assignment based on their current knowledge, their marked-up peer reviews, and their additions and refinements to the document resulting from research and written literature reviews.

Math teachers commonly tell students, "Don't just give the answers—show your work." *Integrated Reading and Writing* is built around the same assumption—writing students must show their work as it progresses into a final draft that is both well-crafted and uniquely their own.

---

[4] See *MLA Handbook* 2.1—2.8 for guidelines on how to avoid plagiarism or check the Purdue OWL at https://owl.english.purdue.edu/owl/.

SECTION I:
COLLEGE WRITING TECHNIQUES

CHAPTER 1: NARRATIVE

Narrative writing simply describes things as they are using agreed-upon facts. It answers these questions:

Questions	Sample Answers
Who was involved?	Zeke
What happened?	Started coloring
When did it happen?	When he was five years old
Where did it happen?	In kindergarten at school
Why did it happen?	In obedience to Miss Miller
How did it happen?	Using a new box of crayons

The person who writes narrative works like a building's plumbing that does not influence the temperature or quality of the water. Plumbing merely delivers water. Users may conclude that "the water is hot," or "the water stinks," or "the water is delicious," but they are drawing their own conclusions based on successful delivery of facts by invisible yet essential plumbing. Writers who remain equally invisible achieve objectivity. Consider the differences between objective and subjective information:

Opinion: Yesterday it was cold outside.

Fact: Yesterday morning it was minus three degrees Fahrenheit outside.

Opinions are often so well accepted that they are recognized as fact but need to be talked about in objective ways so the audience is more receptive to the message:

Opinion: Jesus Christ is the Son of God.

Fact: Jesus Christ *said* he was the Son of God.

Attribution is the art of assigning all subjective information to its source and permitting readers to draw their own conclusions. The statement may or may not be fact, but it is a fact that the statement was made.

Fact: noun—truth; reality; a thing known for certain to have occurred or to be true; a datum of experience, events, or circumstances as distinct from its legal interpretation.

Bias: verb—cause to swerve from a course; influence (usually unfairly), inspire with prejudice. The art of narrative writing is to present facts in an unbiased way. The next chapter deals with descriptive writing, and it is important to recognize the differences now.

Subjective presentation of information is often used in descriptive writing, the subject of the next chapter.

Objective presentation of information works well in
narrative writing, the subject of this chapter.

ASSIGNMENT

Find a newspaper article containing only unbiased
narrative. Hint: It will probably be in the news section
rather than on the editorial or sports pages. Use the
distinctions given here:

Subjective	Objective
(descriptive writing)	(narrative writing)
Opinion: Exists only in the mind	Fact: Exists in nature. Known object.
Personal judgment	Real, outside of the mind
Result of feelings or temperament	Actual, independent of mind
Incapable of being checked externally or verified by other people	Without bias or prejudice
	Detached, impersonal

Narrative writing simply describes things as they are
using agreed-upon facts. Do not imagine narrative to be
inherently boring. Narrative has a purpose and makes a
point, often by portraying action and conflict as in this

oral tradition story told by Blessings Chagomerana in Malawi, Africa:

Akafula for Short

A long time ago in Nyasaland a group of people called Akafula always fought against the Chewa and Ngoni. At the beginning the Chewa people came here from Zaire because of war. The Ngoni people also came here and they were all living together as one.

The Chewa were like kings because they were the first to come, but there were no problems with the Ngoni…. Then the Akafula came to Nyasaland, but instead of just living as friends, they started fighting.

The Akafuna were very short—no more than one and one-half meters tall—and they did not want to be under the leadership of the Chewa. They would always fight other people. For example, if an Akafula person was walking along the way and met someone not from his tribe, he would ask, "How far away did you see me?"

If you answered, "I did not see you until we came very close together," then the Akafula would fight you for insulting him for being so short. But if you said, "I saw you coming from far away," then you would have honored him for being tall and that might have kept him from fighting you…. Now days if someone is very short, people will say they are Akafula as a way of mocking them. (23-24)

Notice that the African story teller used dialogue to spice up a narrative. With this technique, opinion can slip through because it is attributed to a source other than the author. To write, "the dog is ugly," reveals author bias, but to write, "Maria said, 'the dog is ugly,'" maintains author objectivity.

NARRATIVE READING

Narrative writing derives from the oral tradition of storytelling. Note in the story below how carefully the narrator avoids expressing opinion and merely reports facts. Whenever an opinion is expressed, it is attributed to—and spoken by—one of the characters. Writers skilled in the art of attribution are able to present a story objectively while showing how the people influenced by the events of the narrative feel about what happens.

Ruth 1-4

A long time ago, when judges still ruled *over Israel* and the land was dried up with famine, a man from Bethlehem, *which ironically means "place of bread,"* left his home in Judah to live as a foreigner in the land of

21

Moab. He traveled with his wife and their two sons. [2] His name was Elimelech, and his wife was Naomi; their two sons were called Mahlon and Chilion. They were *descendants* of Ephraim's tribe from Bethlehem in Judah. They had settled and made lives for themselves in Moab, [3] but *soon after,* Elimelech died leaving Naomi in the care of her sons. [4] Each son married a woman from Moab—one was named Orpah, the other Ruth—and they lived together for 10 years [5] before Mahlon and Chilion died also. Naomi was left alone, without her husband and two sons.

[6-7] Word had reached Moab that the Eternal One had *once again brought life back to the land of Israel and* blessed His people with food. Naomi prepared to return with her daughters-in-law. With Orpah and Ruth at her side, she began her journey back to Judah, leaving the place where she had lived.

Naomi *(to Orpah and Ruth)***:** [8] *You have accompanied me far enough;* you must both return *to Moab.* Go home to your mothers' care *and your people.* May the Eternal show His loyal love to you just as you demonstrated it to my dead *sons* and me. [9] I hope He will bring you new husbands and that you will find the rest *you deserve* in their homes.

She *drew close,* kissed them, *and turned to go on her way, alone.* But Orpah and Ruth wailed and sobbed, crying out to her.

Orpah and Ruth: [10] *Do not leave us!* We insist you take us with you to *live with you and* your people.

Naomi: [11] Go back *to your homes,* my daughters. What possible reason would you have for returning with me? Do you think there are more sons inside of me? Will you marry these unborn sons? [12] *Listen to me,* daughters, and go back. I am too old; I will not marry again *because I cannot conceive. But even if I could*—if I still believed there was hope for me, or if I had a husband and conceived sons tonight— [13] would you *waste a lifetime* waiting for them to grow up? Would you let this *hope for the future* keep you from remarrying *now*? Of course not, my *dear* daughters. It is obvious that the Eternal has acted against me. My life is much too bitter for you to share with me.

[14] At this Orpah and Ruth wailed and wept again. Then Orpah kissed Naomi, *said goodbye, and returned the way she had come.* Yet Ruth refused to let go of Naomi.

Naomi: [15] Look at your sister-in-law. She has returned to *live with* her people and to *worship* her gods; go and follow her.

¹⁶ **Ruth:** Stop pushing me away,

insisting that I stop following you!

Wherever you go, I will go.

Wherever you live, I will live.

Your people will be my people.

Your God will be my God.

¹⁷ Wherever you die, I will also die

and be buried there *near you.*

May the Eternal One punish me—

and even more so—

if anything besides death comes between us.

¹⁸ When Naomi *heard this and* saw Ruth's resolve, she stopped trying to talk her out of returning *to Judah.*

¹⁹ The two women went on together to Bethlehem. News of their arrival spread throughout Bethlehem. In fact, the whole community was humming with the report, with the women exclaiming, "Could it really be *the same* Naomi *who left us so long ago?*"

²⁰ **Naomi:** Do not call me Naomi *ever again, for I am no longer pleasant.* Call me Mara *instead, for I am filled with bitterness* because the Highest One has treated me bitterly. I left this place full, *in spite of the famine,* but the Eternal has brought me back empty *from a plentiful land.* Why would you call me "Pleasant" when the

Eternal has testified against me, and the Highest One has brought disaster upon me?

²² This was how Naomi came into Bethlehem with her daughter-in-law, Ruth, from Moab. It was at the beginning of the barley harvest when they returned *to the land*.

2 Now Naomi's *deceased* husband, Elimelech, had a relative *in Bethlehem,* an *honorable,* wealthy man named Boaz. ² One day Ruth (the *foreign* woman *who returned with Naomi* from Moab) approached Naomi with a request.

Ruth: Let me go out into the field and pick up whatever grain is left behind *the harvesters*. Maybe someone will be merciful to me.

Naomi: Go ahead, my daughter.

³ Ruth left and went into the fields to pick up the gleanings, *the grain that had been* left behind by the harvesters. And so it was that the portion of the field she was working in belonged to Boaz, who was a part of Elimelech's family.

⁴ *As she was working in his field,* Boaz happened to arrive from Bethlehem, and he greeted the harvesters.

Boaz: The Eternal One be with you.

Harvesters: May the Eternal bless you!

[5] Then *seeing Ruth,* Boaz spoke to the young man in charge of the harvesters.

Boaz: Whom does this young woman belong to?

Overseer: [6] She is the Moabite woman who came back with Naomi from Moab. [7] She came and asked my permission to pick up the grain our harvesters leave behind and gather *it all into sheaves for herself.* Except for one small break she has been here all day, working *in the field* from the morning until now.

Boaz *(to Ruth)***:** [8] Listen to me, my daughter. Do not go and glean in any other field. In fact, do not go outside my property at all but stay with the young women who work for me *following the harvesters and bundling the grain into sheaves.* [9] Watch the harvesters, and see which field they are working in. Follow along behind these servants of mine. I have warned the young men not to touch you. If you are thirsty, go and get a drink from the water jars my young men have filled *for the harvesters.*

[10] *Overwhelmed,* Ruth bowed down *before Boaz,* putting her face to the ground *in front of him.*

Ruth: I am just a foreigner. Why have you noticed me and treated me as if I'm one of your favorites?

Boaz: [11] I have heard your story. I know about everything you have done for your mother-in-law since your own husband died. I know you left your own mother and father, *your home and* your country, and you have come to live in a culture that must seem strange to you. [12] May the Eternal repay you *for your sacrifices* and reward you richly for what you have done. It is under the wings of Israel's God, the Eternal One, that you have sought shelter.

Ruth: [13] I pray you will continue to look upon me with such favor, my lord. I am comforted by your kind words, even though I am not *as worthy of them* as even one of your servant girls.

[14] *Later* during the meal, Boaz spoke to Ruth *again*.

Boaz: Come over here and have some of my food. Dip your piece of bread in the vinegar wine.

So Ruth sat down among the harvesters. Boaz also offered her some roasted grain. She ate as much as she wanted and even had some left over. [15] *When her meal was finished,* she got back up and returned to work. Then Boaz *pulled some of* the young harvesters aside and gave them instructions *about her.*

Boaz: Let her pick up grain from among the sheaves. Do not reprimand *or humiliate* her *for gleaning where it is usually forbidden.* [16] Instead, periodically pick out a stalk or two from the sheaves that have already been bound, and leave them for her to gather *for herself.* Make sure that no one gives her a hard time.

[17] So Ruth worked in the field *all day* until the sun had nearly set. *When she finished picking up the leftover ears,* she beat her gathered *barley* grains *from the stalks with a stick. All that work* resulted in over 20 quarts of grain. [18] Then she carried it back to the city where her mother-in-law saw how much she had gleaned. Ruth took out the leftover food from what she could not eat *of her midday meal* and gave it to Naomi.

Naomi *(to Ruth)*: [19] Where did you go to work today? Where did you glean *all this from*? *May God* bless the person who gave you this kind of attention.

So Ruth told Naomi *the story of all that had happened to her that day and* on whose land she had worked.

Ruth: The man I worked with today is named Boaz.

Naomi: [20] May the Eternal bless this man. He has not given up showing His *covenant* love toward the living and the dead.

This man is *closely* related to us—he is a kinsman-redeemer of our family.

Ruth: [21] That is not all he did. Boaz also instructed me to stay with his *young* workers for the remainder of his grain harvesting season.

Naomi: [22] It is best that you *do as he says*. Stay with his young women *who bind the sheaves. They will keep you* safe from the hostility and danger of working in another's field.

[23] So *that is what Ruth did.* She kept close to Boaz's young female servants and picked up everything they dropped. *She worked hard* throughout the *seven weeks of the* wheat and barley seasons until the harvest was complete *in early summer.* And *this whole time* she lived at her mother-in-law's home.

3 **Naomi** *(to Ruth)*: My child, it is my responsibility to find a *husband and* place of rest for you—a place where you will find *rest and* contentment. [2] You have been *working* alongside the young women who serve Boaz. Is he not a part of our family? *Early* this evening, *during the late afternoon wind,* he will be on the threshing floor winnowing the barley.

[3] Bathe and perfume yourself. Put on your best dress, then go down onto the threshing floor. *Be careful, though.* Don't let him know you are there until he has finished eating and drinking. [4] *Once he is relaxed,* he will lie down *to sleep.* Make sure you notice where he is. Once he has lain down, go to him. Uncover his feet and lie down. He will tell you what to do.

Ruth: [5] I will do everything you have told me to do.

[6] So she went down to the threshing floor and followed through with everything her mother-in-law told her to

do. [7] Not much later, Boaz finished eating and drinking and was in good spirits. He made his way to the end of a pile of grain and lay down there *to sleep*. Then *very quietly,* Ruth snuck *to where he was lying down.* She uncovered his feet and lay down *at his feet.* [8] *Later, sometime* in the middle of the night, Boaz was startled *and woke up.* When he rolled over *and looked around,* he discovered there was a woman lying at his feet!

Boaz: [9] Who are you?

Ruth: I am your servant Ruth. Spread out *the hem of* your garment so that it covers your servant. You are a near relative *of our family.*

Boaz: [10] May the Eternal bless you, my daughter, for the loyal love you are showing now is even greater than what you showed before. You have not pursued a younger man—either a rich one or a poor one. [11] *You may rest easy.* You have nothing to fear, my child. I will do everything you ask. Everyone in this city agrees you are a woman of virtuous character. [12] You are right that I am in line as a near relative *of your family.* But *I am not the only one, nor the most likely.* There is another man who is more closely related to you than I am.

Boaz: [13] Spend the rest of the night here. In the morning, *I will give* him the chance to *act as your kinsman-redeemer and* redeem you *and your family.* If he is willing to do this, good. But if he is not willing to fulfill his responsibility, then as the Eternal One lives, *I promise* I will redeem *your family by marrying* you. Now remain here until morning comes.

[14] So Ruth lay at his feet until *early* morning—then she got up *to leave while it was still dark,* before she could be recognized by anyone, because Boaz realized no one should know the woman was on the threshing room floor.

Boaz: [15] Now bring me the outer garment you are wearing. Hold it out, *and hold on tightly.*

She did so, and Boaz filled her garment with six measures of barley grain. He handed it to her; then he *left her and* went into the town *to conduct his business.*

[16] When Ruth returned to Naomi's home, her mother-in-law asked her daughter what happened. Ruth related all that Boaz had *said and* done.

Ruth: [17] He even gave me these six measures of barley grain saying to me, "You can't go back to your mother-in-law empty-handed."

Naomi: [18] Now you must wait, daughter. *We must wait and* see what happens. *Be at peace.* That man will not rest today until this is resolved.

4 At that same time, Boaz went to the *city* gate and he sat down. Just then, the kinsman-redeemer *of the family* he had told *Ruth* about walked by.

Boaz: My friend, come and sit down with me *for awhile. We have some business.*

So the man came and sat down *beside Boaz.* [2] *Before he spoke further to the man,* he gathered together 10 elders from the city and asked them to preside there, which they did.

Boaz *(to the kinsman-redeemer)*: [3] You have heard of Naomi? She is the woman who *recently* returned from Moab. She is transferring her rights to the plot of land belonging to *her deceased husband*—our relative—Elimelech. [4] I wanted you to know about it *because as a close family member, you have the first right to* purchase it. *If you want to do so,* we have enough elders sitting here to witness the transaction. If you want to *become the guardian and* redeem this land, it is yours. But if you are not interested in doing this, tell me *now*. The right belongs to you, *but if you refuse it,* I am next in line.

Kinsman-Redeemer: *Of course,* I exercise my option to redeem this land.

Boaz: [5] Now, *just so you know,* on the day you buy this *plot of* land [from Naomi, you will also acquire Ruth the Moabitess; she is] the dead man's widow. *It will be your*

32

responsibility to make sure she has children so that they can carry on her dead husband's name with the inheritance.

Kinsman-Redeemer: [6] Then I will not be able to redeem it. I will not put my own property at risk. I relinquish my right to redeem the land. You do it.

[7] Now in the old days of Israel *when this story was playing out,* land was redeemed and *property was* transferred legally when a man *involved in the sale* removed one of his sandals and gave it to the other. This was how contracts were sealed in Israel. [8] So the kinsman-redeemer took off his sandal *and handed it to Boaz.*

Kinsman-Redeemer: It's now your responsibility.

Boaz *(to the elders and all the people)*: [9] Every one of you have witnessed *what happened here* today. I secured the rights to everything that belonged to Elimelech and *his sons,* Mahlon and Chilion, from Naomi. [10] I have also taken responsibility for Ruth—the woman from Moab who was married to Mahlon. She will become my wife. I will see to it that his family and this city remember Mahlon. I will *raise children who will bear his name and* make sure his property stays in the family. You are all witnesses *to this* today.

Elders and People: [11] We are witnesses *of what has happened here today*. May the Eternal take this woman who is becoming a part of your family *today* and make her like Rachel and Leah, the two women responsible for building the nation of Israel *with their children*. And may your reputation become well known and well respected throughout Ephrathah and Bethlehem. [12] May the children the Eternal gives you and this woman make your family like the family of Perez, who was born from *a Levirate union between* Judah and Tamar.

[13] Then Boaz took *responsibility of* Ruth, and they married. After they came together, Ruth conceived by the Eternal's provision, and *later* she gave birth to a son.

Women *(to Naomi)***:** [14] Praise the Eternal One. *He has not abandoned you*. He did not leave you without a redeeming guardian. May your offspring become famous all through Israel. [15] May this child give you a new life. May he *strengthen you and* provide for you in your old age. Look at your daughter-in-law, Ruth. She loves you. *This one devoted daughter* is better to you than seven sons would be. She is the one who gave you this child.

[16] Then Naomi held the child tightly in her arms and cared for him. [17] All around her, friends cried out, "Naomi has a son!" They named the child Obed *because he would provide for his grandmother*. Obed *grew up*

and became the father of Jesse. Jesse, too, became *a father one day,* the father of David.

[18] Here is the genealogy of Perez's family: Perez was Hezron's father. [19] Hezron was Ram's father. Ram was Amminadab's father. [20] Amminadab was Nahshon's father. Nahshon was Salmon's father. [21] Salmon was Boaz's father. Boaz was Obed's father. [22] Obed was Jesse's father. And Jesse was the father of David.

ANALYSIS QUESTIONS

Write a paragraph of response to each question below. The questions are designed to introduce you to the art of literary criticism and analysis using Bloom's Taxonomy, which provides opportunity to demonstrate your knowledge, comprehension, application, analysis, synthesis, and evaluation of the reading model (Dalton).

Write your responses in the form of a letter or casual conversation with the author of the narrative. It may be easier if you imagine the author is a personal friend, relative, or college roommate. Your responses will serve as a form of pre-writing to help you master narrative style and prepare you to write a narrative of your own.

1. Search for a spot in the narrative where the author expresses an opinion. If you can find such an

expression, explain whether it is appropriate or inappropriate given the context.

2. What is Ruth's opinion of Boaz? How do you know?

3. What is Naomi's opinion of Ruth? How do you know?

4. What do you think is the author's purpose in narrating the story of Ruth?

5. Showing action is important in many narratives. In your opinion, what is the most exciting action that takes place in this story? Give details. Why do you like it?

6. What are the issues behind the main conflict in this narrative? Give details.

7. From what point of view is this story told? How would the story feel differently if it were told from the point of view of Boaz?

8. Dialogue is used in this story to reveal character. In what ways do you feel you know Ruth better because you have "heard" her talk?

9. What techniques of narrative writing have you learned from Ruth that may be useful for writing your own narrative?

10. Find any news article online and compare it with this story. What is the bias of each author? (See *MLA Handbook* 5.4.5 for how to document a newspaper

article; see *MLA Handbook* 6.4.8 for how to document a Bible passage.)

WRITING ASSIGNMENT

It is time to write your own narrative. Write this paper on a topic about which you are passionate. This topic will most likely fall within the area of your academic major. For example, most psychology majors are particularly interested in a specific psychological phenomenon. Natural science majors want to study biology, or chemistry, or geology, or physics. Music students may be focused on Baroque or Jazz or another genre of music, or on a favorite composer. If you have not declared a major, focus on something you could enjoy studying in great depth—a favorite thing to think about—a topic so fascinating you could write 35 pages without getting *bored*. Identify your topic here:

_____

_____

_____

As you write, follow these guidelines:

1. A narrative relates a series of events. **Assignment:** Write a narrative containing a series of events that influenced you to embrace the interest that you have.

2. A narrative makes a point or has a purpose.

   Assignment: State the purpose of your narrative.

3. Action plays a central role in any narrative.

   Assignment: Show lots of action in your narrative.

4. A narrative needs a point of view. **Assignment:** Even though the narrative is about yourself, adopt a third-person point of view as your narrative style. Follow the example of the Ruth narrative.

5. Good narrative uses dialogue. **Assignment:** Include at least one brief conversation using quote marks and paragraphing as modeled in the *MLA Handbook* (look up "quotes" in the index for guidelines on how to format and punctuate dialogue). Remember: the narrative itself must be objective, but subjective material can be attributed to a character who expresses opinion in the form of dialogue.

6. Now imagine you are talking to a stranger who knows little about your topic. Use very simple language to explain your topic to that person. Answer the journalist's questions in your narrative: who, what, when, where, why, how?

7. Write a one-page narrative based on what you already know about the topic.

If you had trouble with this exercise or discovered that you want to write about something not within your college major, do not panic. Remember, "We have different gifts, according to the grace given us. . . . [Let us] use it in proportion to [our] faith" (Rom. 12:6). Alexander Borodin was a nineteenth-century Russian composer, a member of "The Mighty Handful," a group of composers dedicated to producing Russian music. His opera, *Prince Igor*, is thought by some to have been his most significant work, but Borodin was an organic chemist! He considered himself merely a "Sunday composer" ("AlexanderBorodin").

Similarly, Socrates was a stonemason who asked questions and challenged people to think. Today he is remembered as the founder of Western philosophical thought (Carr). Alexander Graham Bell was a teacher whose wife was nearly deaf, and he invented the telephone trying to help her hear better ("Alexander Graham Bell"). The Wright brothers built bicycles in Ohio but fiddled around with the idea of flying—just as a sideline ("The Wright Story").

You are a complex person with many talents and interests. You have no idea what you will become. But one way to get there is to begin now using God-given talents to write concerning things you are passionate about. What is your deepest dream? Write a narrative concerning that dream—even if you presume that achieving it is impossible.

PEER REVIEW

Valuable insights often result when a fellow student reads and evaluates the narrative. Even readers who are not qualified as editors can serve as an audience for the narrative, and their responses can help the author make refinements.

_____ The entire narrative must be written from the third-person point of view. Circle all first and second person pronouns and make suggestions to help the writer get it all in third person.

Avoid 1ST Person Pronouns: I, me, my, we, us, our

Avoid   2nd Person Pronouns: you, your, y'all

Use 3rd Person Pronouns: he, she, him, her, they, them, their, those

Hint: One easy way to write in third person is to choose plural subjects for sentences so third person plural pronouns can be used. **Example:** Instead of "The <u>child</u> takes <u>his/her</u> lunch to school in a sack," write "The <u>children</u> take <u>their</u> lunches to school in sacks."

_____ Search through the narrative again, this time looking for evidence that all six questions have been adequately answered (who, what, when, where, why, how?).

_____ Evaluate the structure to make sure the six questions have been answered in the order the reader is likely to ask them. Also, some of the questions get answered over and over again at increasing levels of significance.

_____ "Place brackets [ ] to identify all dialogue," he suggested, "and make sure quote marks and punctuation are done correctly." (See MLA 3.7.7 "Punctuation with Quotations" for guidelines.)

_____ Identify incorrect use of commas so the author can make corrections (See MLA 3.2.2 "Commas" for guidelines).

Answer the following questions:

What is the main point of this narrative?

_____

What is the biggest strength?

_____

What material does not fit the main point or the audience?

_____

What questions has the author not answered?

_____

At what point does the paper fail to hold my interest?

_____

Why?

_____

Where is the organization confusing?

_____

Where is the writing unclear or vague?

_____

On the back of your classmate's paper, write a note to the author explaining what you enjoyed most about reading this narrative.

Research Time

_____ Where should more facts be added to give this paper more credibility?

_____ Suggest a source where this author might look up more information that would strengthen the content of this paper.

_____ Write a few reasons why this paper would be better if it had the facts and information suggested in the above questions.

PLANNING THE REWRITE

The first draft seldom reflects a writer's best work. The peer review usually reveals a few ways the first draft can be improved. Consider the suggestions of the peer reviewer, and also read *MLA Handbook* 1.9 "Writing Drafts" and 3.1-3.8 "The Mechanics of Writing" for rewriting suggestions.

Write the final draft on computer and format it according to instructions in the *MLA Handbook* Chapter 4: "The Format of the Research Paper" with header and page number, title, double spacing, and other exact details. Use a Times New Roman 12-point font and one-inch margins. Finally, locate additional information that will strengthen the content of the paper while providing facts and sources that will enhance your credibility. Writing a literature review as explained below will create the research needed.

LITERATURE REVIEW

Add in-depth details to your narrative following these guidelines: Go to the reference desk of your library and locate a *subject* (specialized) encyclopedia specific to the topic of your paper. Locate an article on your topic and fill in the information requested below:

Author (if given): _____

Title of article: _____

Title of Encyclopedia: _____

Call Number of Encyclopedia: _____

Is there a bibliography at the end of the article?

_____ yes _____ no

Read the entries related to your topic in the reference book you have chosen and take notes useful to the paper. Use this information to create a literature review by indirect and direct quotations as explained below.

An **indirect quotation** presents an author's ideas through *paraphrasing* or *summarizing*. **Example**: Ending a sentence with a preposition is an older rule that has, to some extent, been done away with (Strunk and White 77). The idea has been rewritten in words not used by the original author, so it must be referenced. Using indirect quotations indicates that the author clearly understands the information and can smoothly integrate it into an argument.

44

Paraphrasing means rewriting someone else's idea using different words. A paraphrase is usually about the same length as the original. Compare the Living Bible paraphrase with The VOICE translation: "And the Holy Spirit helps us in our distress. For we don't even know what we should pray for, nor how we should pray. But the Holy Spirit prays for us with groanings that cannot be expressed in words" (Rom. 8:26 LB). The above paraphrase gets across the same idea as the following careful translation from the Greek: "A similar thing happens *when we pray*. We are weak and do not know how to pray, so the Spirit steps in and articulates prayers for us with groaning too profound for words" (Rom. 8:26 The VOICE).

Summarizing is a form of indirect quotation, but is much shorter than the original text. A summary encapsulates the essence or main point. **Example:** The Apostle Paul argues in Romans 8:26 that the Holy Spirit mysteriously helps believers to pray effectively.

A **direct quotation** transcribes an author's words from the text using the *exact* wording (including mistakes). Use direct quotations sparingly—only when they make a precise point and are both brief and substantial. **Example:** "Years ago, students were warned not to end a sentence with a preposition; time, of course, has softened that rigid decree" (Strunk and White 77).

Now that the differences are clear between indirect quotation (paraphrasing and summarizing) and direct quotation, do the following:

1. **Paraphrase** a key paragraph of the article being careful to avoid plagiarism as explained in the *MLA Handbook* 2.5.

2. **Summarize** the article or a key part of the article entirely in your own words.

3. **Quote** one excellent sentence by carefully copying it into your paper. Put quote marks around the quote and insert an appropriate introduction such as, Blanchard writes, "Never eat olives after midnight or you'll get cramps."

To find out what information to put in a Works Cited entry to accompany the above paraphrase, summary, and quote, look up "encyclopedia articles" in the index of the *MLA Handbook* (page 273). The index entry will refer you to other sections of the *MLA Handbook* (in this case page 160, "An Article in a Reference Book.") When you have found the correct format to follow, write the information from your article into a Works Cited entry at the end of your paper *in exactly the correct format*.

PARENTHETICAL REFERENCE

Now look at the *MLA* index to find the entry concerning "encyclopedia articles . . . in parenthetical references" and "encyclopedias, as reference sources" to find out how to create a parenthetical reference for your indirect and direct quotes. Insert the parenthetical references at the end of your paraphrase, summary, and quote *in the correct format*.

Guidelines on how to gracefully integrate the new research with the paper you have written are provided in chapter six of the *MLA Handbook*. Pay particular attention to section 6.3 beginning on page 216. In addition to those instructions, be sure to create a context that shows the reader precisely how this new material is an integral part of your paper.

Include a Works Cited page with your paper. The format should use double spacing, hanging indentation, alphabetical order, and look exactly like the Works Cited page at the end of this book. Note that although you will have three or more parenthetical references in the body of your paper, there will be only one Works Cited entry, since all your parenthetical references are to that one source.

When you have made all the needed corrections to your paper, when it is typed without errors and formatted according to MLA guidelines, when you can genuinely say you are proud of this writing—this piece of yourself—and (of course) when the teacher says it is due, turn in the narrative for evaluation and grading. No matter what grade the manuscript receives, celebrate the fact that with your words you have spoken a new creation into existence, and you can savor its beauty and appreciate its goodness.[5]

---

[5] Gen. 1:31: "Then God surveyed everything He had made, savoring *its beauty and appreciating* its goodness."

CHAPTER 2: DESCRIPTION

Narrative writing, explored in the previous chapter, is efficient and respectable as it tells a story and lets the facts speak. Good writers master the art of narrative, and also know when to go beyond it with description. **Descriptive writing** takes a pause in the narrative to look in detail at a particular feature. It can bore or inspire the reader depending on the author's skill. Edward George Bulwer-Lytton's character Pelham plunges into description as he attempts to capture the beauty of a woman he eventually marries:[6]

Never had I seen any countenance half so lovely. She was apparently about twenty, her hair was of the richest chestnut, and a golden light played through its darkness, as if a sunbeam had been caught in those luxuriant tresses, and was striving in vain to escape. Her eyes were of a light hazel, large, deep, and *shaded into softness* (to use a modern expression) by

---

[6] Published in 1828, *Pelham* was a popular English novel that introduced to society dark evening wear for men (the tuxedo). Archaic punctuation in this quote is maintained exactly as the original, even though it does not reflect current MLA or APA style.

long and very dark lashes. Her complexion alone would have rendered her beautiful, it was so clear— so pure; the blood blushed beneath it, like roses under a clear stream; if, in order to justify my simile, roses would have the complacency to grow in such a situation. Her nose was of that fine and accurate mould that one so seldom sees, except in the Grecian statues, which unites the clearest and most decided outline with the most feminine delicacy and softness, and the short curved arch which descended from thence to her mouth, was so fine—so *airily* and exquisitely formed, that it seemed as if Love himself had modelled the bridge which led to his most beautiful and fragrant island. On the right side of the mouth was one dimple, that corresponded so exactly with every smile and movement of those rosy lips, that you might have sworn the shadow of each passed there; it was like the rapid changes of an April heaven reflected upon a valley. She was somewhat, but not much taller, than the ordinary height; and her figure, which united all the first freshness and youth of the girl, with the more luxuriant graces of the woman, was rounded and finished so justly—so *minutely*—that the eye could glance over the whole, without discovering the least harshness, or unevenness, or atom, to be added or subtracted. But over all these was a light, a glow, a pervading spirit, of which it is impossible to convey the faintest idea. You should have seen her by the side of a shaded fountain on a summer's day. You should have watched her amidst music and flowers.... (166-167)

The art of description is to know when enough is enough. If the reader begs, "Please!—get on with the story," the author is using too much description. If the reader smiles and thinks, "I love it when we stop and smell the roses," this author has fostered the intended vicarious experience.

Descriptive writing can also sprinkle itself throughout narrative with carefully placed adjectives (describing words). Profane and vulgar terms are adjectives, and students often ask if such words are appropriate in academic writing. The answer is "no," and authors who stoop to such language are frequently abandoning the creative instinct. A better model is Mark Twain's technique in *Life on the Mississippi* of simulating such language: [7]

---

[7] Note that although MLA specifies that "whang" should use double quote marks, single marks are used here to faithfully reproduce the original text.

All of a sudden, on a murky night, a light would hop up, right under our bows, almost, and an agonized voice, with the backwoods 'whang' to it, would wail out—

'War'n the—you goin' to! Cain't you see nothin', you dash-dashed aig-suckin', sheep-stealin', one-eyed son of a stuffed monkey!' (71-72)

Notice that Twain is using slang to achieve his vulgarity objectives. This is the creative and acceptable alternative to using profanity. In "A Defence of Slang" G. K. Chesterton writes that slang is metaphor: "If we … examine the cheapest cant phrases that pass our lips every day, we should find that they were as rich and suggestive as so many sonnets" (146). Be sure to explain the meaning of slang expressions within the context, as John Bunyan does in *The Holy War*. When Lord Willbewill apprehends Evil-questioning, the villain is entertaining four "doubters" described as "down boys, you have the very length of my foot." This expression is interpreted in the next phrase when Evil-questioning admits that the doubters "are one with my heart" (248).

Simulated profanity can also be handled using adjectives the way Hemingway does in *For Whom the Bell Tolls* when the barbarous "woman of Pablo" says to the gypsy, "What are you doing now, you lazy drunken obscene unsayable son of an unnameable unmarried gypsy obscenity?" (34). Whether in separate passages of description or in adjective-laced narrative, descriptive writing uses all five senses: taste, touch, smell, sight, and sound.

Descriptive writing is particularly effective when many sensations flood together so that the reader seems to *taste* colors, *feel* music, *smell* anger, *see* ideas, or *hear* the sunset. "Synaesthesia" is "The production of a mental sense-impression relating to one sense by the stimulation of another sense, as in coloured hearing. Also, a sensation produced in one part of the body by stimulation of another part." In linguistics it is possible to transfer "the meaning of a word from one kind of sensory experience to another" (OED).

Descriptive writing works to trigger synaesthesia. In a long passage describing steamboat racing in *Life on the Mississippi*, Mark Twain achieves synaesthesia when he describes a frantic scene obscured by clouds of words: "Drays and baggage-vans were clattering hither and thither in a wild hurry, every now and then getting blocked and jammed together, and then during ten seconds one could not see them for the profanity…" (116).

The art of descriptive writing is beautifully illustrated in *Teaching a Stone to Talk* where Annie Dillard relates her experience near the Napo River in the Ecuadorian jungle: "Green fireflies spattered lights across the air and illumined for seconds, now here, now there, the pale trunks of enormous, solitary trees. Beneath us the brown Napo River was rising, in all silence; it coiled up the sandy bank and tangled its foam in vines that trailed from the forest and roots that looped the shore" (54). Having described the setting, Dillard now immerses her reader in a powerful experience of touch:

> Later that night I loosed my hair from its braids and combed it smooth—not for myself, but so the village girls could play with it in the morning.... I had slumped on some shaded steps, wishing I knew some Spanish or some Quechua so I could speak with the ring of little girls who were alternately staring at me and smiling at their toes. I spoke anyway, and fooled with my hair, which they were obviously dying to get their hands on, and laughed, and soon they were all braiding my hair, all five of them, all fifty fingers, all my hair, even my bangs. And then they took it apart and did it again, laughing, and

teaching me Spanish nouns, and meeting my eyes and each other's with open delight.... (54-55)

The reader who wants to get his own hands into Annie's hair has been seduced by wonderful descriptive writing that embraces the senses. Seduction? Yes, and also a taste of heaven as C. S. Lewis explains in *Letters to Malcolm: Chiefly on Prayer*:

But for our body one whole realm of God's glory—all that we receive through the senses—would go unpraised. For the beasts can't appreciate it and the angels are, I suppose, pure intelligences. They *understand* colours and tastes better than our greatest scientists; but have they retinas or palates? I fancy the 'beauties of nature'[8] are a secret God has shared with us alone. That may be one of the reasons why we were made—and why the resurrection of the body is an important doctrine. (17-18)

At the conclusion of his last book, C. S. Lewis affirmed, "What the soul cries out for is the resurrection of the senses" (*Letters to Malcolm* 121). If the five senses are to play such a vital role in human life eternally, surely they should be embraced in the

---

[8] The single quote marks around "beauties of nature" reflect a practice that persists among British authors although MLA calls for double quote marks.

literature of the present world—especially in writings that anticipate such glory.

DESCRIPTION READINGS

The book of Judges provides a dramatic model for how to follow narrative with description. Notice that chapter four is almost pure narrative, reading much like a news article revealing little bias. By contrast, chapter five celebrates the events of the previous narrative, immersing the reader in descriptions of the sorrow of death and the elation of victory.

Judges 4: Narrative

4 After Ehud died, the people returned to doing what the Eternal said was evil. [2] So the Eternal made them subservient to Jabin, king of Canaan, who ruled from Hazor. Jabin's general was a man named Sisera, who lived in Harosheth-hagoyim.

[3] The people of Israel cried out to the Eternal *again for help*. Since Sisera had 900 iron chariots, he prevailed against and oppressed the Israelites for 20 years.

[4] At that time, Deborah the prophetess, wife of Lappidoth, served as judge over Israel. [5] She used to sit beneath the palm tree of Deborah, situated in the hill country of Ephraim between Ramah and Bethel, and the people would go up to her there to settle disputes. [6] She

urgently sent for Barak, the son of Abinoam, out of Kedesh-naphtali.

Deborah: The Eternal God of Israel commands you: "Go and get into position near Mount Tabor. Take 10,000 soldiers from the tribes of Naphtali and Zebulun. [7] I will draw out Sisera, Jabin's general, to meet you at the wadi Kishon with his chariots and his army, and I will deliver him to you."

Barak *(to Deborah)*: [8] I will do this if you will go with me; but if you won't, then I won't go either.

Deborah: [9] I will certainly go with you, but you should know from the beginning that this battle will not lead to your personal glory. The Eternal has decreed that *the mighty* Sisera will be defeated by a woman.

Then Deborah got up and accompanied Barak to Kedesh. [10] Barak summoned *the tribes of* Naphtali and Zebulun, and they sent 10,000 men to follow him. With Deborah, they went to Kedesh.

[11] Now Heber the Kenite had separated himself from all the other Kenites (the descendants of Hobab, the father-in-law of Moses) and had camped far away, under the great tree at Zaanannim, near Kedesh.

[12] When Sisera *the general* heard that Barak, the son of Abinoam, had gone up *in force* to Mount Tabor, [13] he called out all 900 of his iron chariots, and all the soldiers

who were with him from Harosheth-hagoyim to the wadi Kishon.

Deborah *(to Barak)*: ¹⁴ Get up! For this is the day that the Eternal has given you victory over Sisera. In fact, He has already gone out ahead of you.

So Barak went down from Mount Tabor with 10,000 warriors following. ¹⁵ As Barak *and his forces* watched, the Eternal threw Sisera and all his chariots and his entire army into a panic before them; all Sisera's army died by the sword. Sisera himself climbed down from his chariot and escaped on foot, ¹⁶ while Barak *and his army* pursued Sisera's chariots and army all the way back to Harosheth-hagoyim. All of Sisera's warriors perished by the sword; not one of them was left *alive*.

¹⁷ Sisera had fled to the tent of Jael, the wife of Heber the Kenite, *and he must have thought himself safe at last,* since there was peace between Jabin, the king of Hazor, and Heber the Kenite.

¹⁸ Jael went out to meet Sisera.

Jael: Come in, my lord, come in with me. There is nothing to be afraid of here.

So he came inside the tent with her, and she covered him with a rug *just in case some of Barak's soldiers came looking for him.*

Sisera: ¹⁹ May I have a little water to drink?

He was very thirsty, so she opened a skin filled with milk and gave him a little, then covered him again.

Sisera: [20] Stand *and wait* at the opening to the tent. If anybody comes and asks you, "Is anyone inside?" tell them "No."

[21] Sisera fell into a deep sleep, for he was weary. Jael, the wife of Heber, took a tent peg in one hand and a hammer in the other. She crept softly to his side. Then she drove the peg into his temple, down into the ground, and killed him.

[22] When Barak came looking for Sisera, Jael went out to meet him.

Jael: Come inside, and I will show you the man you seek.

So he went into the tent with her, and there lay Sisera dead, with a tent peg driven through his head.

[23] On that day, God vanquished Jabin, king of Canaan, before the people of Israel; [24] and the Israelites bore down harder and harder on him until at last Jabin, king of Canaan, was destroyed.

ANALYSIS QUESTIONS

1. Discuss the efficiency with which the writer of Judges 4 covers the basic narrative questions of who, what, when, where, why, and how.

2. Suppose that your local newspaper had existed in the time of the Judges. Write a headline for that publication's front story article about this event.
3. Explain the ways a news article would be both similar and different from that reported in Judges 4.

Judges 5: Description *The Song of Deborah*

5 Then, that same day, Deborah and Barak, the son of Abinoam, sang a song *in victory*:

[2] The leaders of Israel stood up,

   and the people offered themselves willingly—

   praise the Eternal One!

[3] Listen, all you kings, and pay attention, you rulers:

   I, I will sing to the Eternal,

   I will sing praise to Him, the True God of Israel!

[4] Eternal One, when You went out from Seir

   and marched from the field of Edom,

The earth shook,

   and the heavens poured;

   yes, the clouds poured water.

[5] The mountains flowed *like water* before the Eternal, the God of Sinai;

   they melted into a flood before the Eternal One, the True God of Israel.

[6] In the days of Shamgar, the son of Anath,

and in the days of Jael, the main roads were empty *of caravans,*

and the travelers kept to back roads.

[7] But those from rural areas stayed away,

the destitute in Israel kept far off,

Until I, Deborah, arose

to be a mother to Israel.

[8] They had chosen new gods,

so war came to their gates.

Was there a spear or shield to be found then

among the 40,000 of Israel?

[9] My heart is warmed by those in Israel called to command them,

who offered themselves willingly to the people.

Praise the Eternal One!

[10] Sing *this song,* those of you who now ride white donkeys

and sit on rich carpets,

you who travel along the road.

[11] All of you who now hear the sound of shepherds at the watering places,

proclaim the just victories of the Eternal,

the just triumphs of His destitute people in Israel,

As the people of the Eternal go down to the gates!

¹² Wake up, wake up, Deborah!

   Wake up, wake up, and sing!

Get up, Barak! *Get up and* carry off your captives,

   O son of Abinoam!

¹³ Then down went a surviving people to those who were noble,

   and the Eternal One marched to me with the mighty!

¹⁴ People with roots in Ephraim went down against the Amalekites after you, O Benjamin,

   with your people.

From Machir marched those commanders,

   and from Zebulun went those carrying the staff of a scribe.

¹⁵ The chiefs of Issachar came with Deborah;

   Issachar was faithful to Barak,

And they rushed into the valley, close at his heels.

   And the clans of Reuben wondered in their heart,

¹⁶ "Why did you remain idle and aloof in the sheepfolds?

   To hear whistling for the flocks?"

And the clans of Reuben wondered in their heart,

¹⁷ "Why did those of Gilead remain beyond the Jordan?

   Why did the people of Dan stay with their ships?

"Why did the people of Asher stay on the coast,

   settling down where they landed?"

¹⁸ But Zebulun did not fear death,

and Naphtali, too, *stared down death* on the heights
where the battle raged.

¹⁹ The kings came, they fought;

the kings of Canaan made war.

They fought at Taanach, by the waters of Megiddo,

but they won no spoils of silver.

²⁰ The stars themselves fought *against them*;

from the heavens, the stars fought against Sisera.

²¹ The raging waters of Kishon swept them away,

the rushing waters, the raging waters of Kishon.

March forward, my soul, march on with strength!

²² The hooves of the horses beat loudly;

the galloping of the horses echoed.

²³ "A curse on Meroz!" said the messenger of the Eternal
One;

"May its people be bitterly cursed,

Because they did not come to help the Eternal,

to stand with the Eternal against the mighty foes!"

²⁴ But Jael,

the wife of Heber, the Kenite—most blessed of
women is she,

favored above all women who dwell in tents!

²⁵ Sisera asked for water, and she gave him milk;

she gave him curds in a dish fit for lords.

²⁶ And then she took a tent peg in her *left* hand

and a worker's hammer in her right,

And she struck Sisera.

She broke and battered his head;

she pierced his temple.

²⁷ At her feet he bowed, he fell,

he dropped silent.

At her feet he fell, he dropped,

and where he dropped, there he lay dead.

²⁸ The mother of Sisera waited for him,

watching through the lattice of the window.

"Why is his chariot so long in returning?" she wondered.

"Where are the hoofbeats of his horses?"

²⁹ Her wisest ladies *in waiting* have answers—

in fact, she herself thinks she knows the reason.

³⁰ "Aren't they still dividing the spoils of a successful battle?

A girl or two given to every man;

Spoils of beautiful dyed cloth for Sisera,

spoils of dyed cloth, beautifully embroidered.

Indeed two pieces of beautiful embroidered cloth for my neck."

³¹ So may all Your enemies perish, O Eternal One!

But may those who love You be like the sun,

rising and going forth with power!

After this victory, the people knew peace *from war* for 40 years.

ANALYSIS QUESTIONS

4. Which of the five senses (taste, touch, smell, sight, sound) is dominant in Deborah's description of the conflict? Speculate on why this may be deliberate.

5. Imagine you are peer reviewing Deborah's description. Which of the five senses do you wish she would explore more thoroughly? Write a sentence that you can recommend for inclusion in case she were to revises her paper.

6. Make a list of at least five ways in which Judges 5 is different from Judges 4.

7. Which version of the conflict do you like better, the narrative in Judges 4, or the more descriptive Song of Deborah in Judges 5? Why?

METAPHOR AS DESCRIPTION

In addition to modeling how to talk about the same event with separate narratives and descriptions, the Bible also uses metaphor to enhance the way a thing is described. A metaphor is a symbol of some other (usually abstract) thing. To say that the university library is a "hive of activity" is a metaphor.[9] Hebrews 1:7 reads, "I make my heavenly messengers like the winds, and My servants like a flame," and verses 10-12 read as follows:

[10] In the beginning, You, Lord, laid the foundation of the earth and set the skies above us with Your own hands. [11] *But while* they will someday pass away, You remain *forever*; when they wear out like old clothes, [12] You will roll them up and change them into something new. But You will never change; Your years will never come to an end.

The writer who combines metaphor with the five senses can stir a reader's soul as in the Song of Songs 2:1-7:

Her: I am a rose of Sharon, a lily *found in one* of the valleys.

[2] **Him:** Like a lily among thorns, that is what she is; my dear is *a captivating beauty* among the young women.

[3] **Her:** My love is like an apple tree in a wooded forest; he is *a ripe tree* among *a grove of saplings,* those young men. I sat beneath his *ample* shade, filled with such joy. I tasted the sweetness of his fruit

---

[9] English teachers often say, "A metaphor is a comparison between two people, places, or things without the use of *like* or *as.*"

and longed for more.

[4] He placed me at his banquet table, *for everyone to see that* his banner over me declares his love.

[5] *(to those around)* Sustain me with *sweet* raisins. Refresh my *energy* with apples because I am lovesick *for him.*

[6] His left hand cradles my head; his right embraces me.

[7] (to the young women) You of Jerusalem *heed my warning.* By the gazelles and deer of the field, I charge you not to excite your love until it is ready. Don't stir *a fire in your heart* too soon, *until it is ready to be satisfied.*

ANALYSIS QUESTIONS

8. The writer might have said his heavenly messengers are "dynamic" but instead says they are "like wind, like a flame." Is this a metaphor, or are they actually flames? No matter which interpretation you choose, what sensory impressions did you experience due to the "wind" and "flame" language? Which style of saying it do you like better? Why?

9. Write a few sentences describing the image that jumped into your mind when you read the metaphor

predicting that the heavens "will wear out like old clothes."

10. Write a one paragraph summary of Song of Songs 2:1-7 in your own words.

WRITING ASSIGNMENT

1. It is time to write your own description on a topic related to the one you used when writing the narrative in chapter one. Your instructor might give you the option of adding a page of description to your previous narrative. If so, highlight or underline the added material so it is clear to the reader what descriptive elements have been added.

2. Description presents impressions. **Assignment:** Use all five senses (taste, touch, smell, sight, sound) in your writing to convey the same sensory impressions for the reader as you experienced when you became passionate about the subject.

3. Adjectives and adverbs add interesting description. (She walked *carefully* over the *slippery* ice). **Assignment:** Without overdoing it, experiment with using carefully chosen adjectives and adverbs in every paragraph.

4. Write your one-page description. Try to capture the sensations that make your topic fascinating. Express

yourself with all five senses: taste, touch, smell, sight, and sound. Make your listener want to love and experience this topic as much as you do.

5. Bring your description to class when it is due for peer-review by a classmate.

PEER REVIEW: It is time to have a fellow student read and evaluate the description paper. The instructor is likely to assign partners for students who have just done the same exercise.

_____ The entire description must be written from the third-person point of view. Circle all the words like "I," "we," and "you" and make suggestions to help the writer get it all in third person.

_____ Sniff through the description again, this time looking for evidence that all five senses are used. Whenever you detect "taste," "touch," "smell," "sight," or "sound," write that word in the margin. Make sure all five senses are used to their full effect.

_____ Review the use of <u>adjectives</u>—*clever* describing words that modify nouns—to make sure they are used effectively. Suggest additional adjectives that might strengthen the paper.

_____ Review the use of <u>adverbs</u>—words that *cleverly* alter the meaning of verbs—to make sure they are used effectively. Suggest additional adverbs that might strengthen the paper.

_____ Underline the <u>verbs</u> in key sentences and contemplate stronger words to portray the same action. Be suspicious of any sentence beginning with "there are" or "it is" as well as excessive use of the word "that." These sentences call for stronger verbs or more precise subjects.

_____ How do you *feel* after reading this description? Have you lost yourself in the description—have you been transported into another world? If not, have you at least caught the author's enthusiasm? If so, what "grabbed" you and effectively communicated this enthusiasm? If not, what suggestions can you give to make it grab you? Write your suggestions on the back of the student's paper.

_____ Review the paper one last time for correct spelling and punctuation. For guidelines, see the *MLA Handbook*

3.1 (spelling) and 3.2 (punctuation). To get some idea of the importance of punctuation, consider which punctuation you agree with in the following sentence:

"A woman, without her man, is nothing."

"A woman: without her, man is nothing" (Truss 13).

Research Time

_____ Where should more facts be added to give this paper more credibility?

_____ Suggest a source where this author might look up more information that would strengthen the content of this paper.

_____ Write a few reasons why this paper would be better if it had the facts and information suggested in the above questions.

PLANNING THE REWRITE

In addition to carefully considering the suggestions of the peer reviewer, read the _MLA Handbook_ 3.1-3.8 "The Mechanics of Writing" and 1.9 "Writing Drafts" for helpful rewriting suggestions. As with the narrative assignment, the final draft of the description should be written on computer and formatted like the sample in the

MLA Handbook page 117 with header, margins, title, double spacing, and other details exactly as modeled.

LITERATURE REVIEW

Add reliable details to your description following these guidelines: Go to the library catalog and locate a <u>book</u> on your topic. Find the book in your library and write down at least one subject heading from the book:

Subject heading _____

Now fill in the information requested below:

Author: _____

Title of book: _____

City of publisher: _____

Name of publisher: _____

Date of publication: _____

Is there a bibliography at the end of the book?

_____ yes _____ no

In the space below, speculate on the potential advantages of reading books in your subject area from highly reputable publishers that also contain a bibliography:

_____

_____

Just as you did on the narrative paper, write a literature review by preparing a paraphrase, summary, and quote from this new source:

1. **Paraphrase** an important section of the book. Be careful to avoid plagiarism as explained in the *MLA Handbook* 2.5.

2. **Summarize** several pages of the book in your own words.

3. **Quote** one excellent example of descriptive writing by copying it carefully into your paper. Put quote marks around the material and insert an appropriate introduction such as, <u>Blanchard writes</u>, "Never eat olives after midnight or you'll get cramps."

To find out what information to put in a Works Cited page to accompany the above paraphrase, summary, and quote, look up "books" in the index of the *MLA Handbook* (page 268). The index entries will refer you to other sections of the *MLA Handbook*. When you find the correct format to follow, write that information in your paper *in the correct format*.

PARENTHETICAL REFERENCE

Look in the *MLA* index to find the entry concerning "books . . . in parenthetical references" to find out how to reference your quote. Insert the parenthetical reference at the end of the above paraphrase, summary, and quote *in the correct format*. Insert the new information from this worksheet into the appropriate places in the final draft of the description.

Guidelines on how to gracefully integrate the new research with the paper you have written are provided in chapter six of the *MLA Handbook*. Pay particular attention to section 6.3 beginning on page 216. In addition to those instructions, be sure to create a context that shows the reader precisely how this new material is an integral part of your paper.

Include a Works Cited page with your paper. The format should use double spacing, hanging indentation, alphabetical order, and look exactly like the Works Cited page at the end of this book, or the samples on page 232 of the *MLA Handbook*.

Tip One: How to use subject pronouns

Academic writing generally favors third person. However, when first person is used, remember that the subject pronouns *I, he, she, it, you, they,* and *we* are always used as subjects. The object pronouns *him, her, me, them,* and *us* are never used as subjects. When a pronoun is part of a compound subject, treat it as the only subject when deciding what pronoun to use. For example, students confused by whether to use *I* or *me* with compound subjects can learn from these examples:

"I like pizza." Therefore, "My wife and I like pizza."
"The pizza belongs to me"(not "I"). Therefore, "The
pizza belongs to my wife and me" (not "I").

Tip Two: When to capitalize proper pronouns

If you can insert the person's name, capitalize the
substituted word: "I said Dad was tall." If you cannot
insert the person's name, do not capitalize: "I said my
dad was tall."

CHAPTER 3: PROCESS

Narrative writing tells a story; descriptive writing adds pizzazz. Another important step is to identify and explain a **process** in a chosen academic discipline. All disciplines follow some sort of **process**. Both medical doctors and auto mechanics perform a *diagnosis* by following an established *process* to decide what is wrong with people and vehicles. Composers have a set of rules to follow when writing each particular variety of music. When Johann Sebastian Bach wrote his *Fugue in G. Minor*, he followed the prescribed pattern for a fugue by starting out with a theme that repeats throughout the composition in different voices (Bach). He knew voices can overlap and invert, and be played backward or repeated.

Process papers explain how a thing happened, or how it can be made to happen. Articles about processes make up the bulk of many professional journals, and one objective of this chapter is to introduce students to the periodical publications in their discipline, and to encourage them to make it a habit to read those magazines and journals.

PROCESS READINGS

Process is an ancient form of writing and appears in a document attributed to Moses (Gen. 6:11-22):

[11-12] *They lived at a time when* the world had become *vile and* corrupt. Violence was everywhere. God saw that the earth was in ruins, *and He knew why:* all people on earth *except Noah* had lived corrupt lives and ruined God's plans for them. *He had to do something.*

Eternal One *(to Noah)***:** [13] *Noah,* I have decided to wipe out all the living creatures *I have made* because they are spreading violence throughout the earth. Watch! I will destroy them with the earth. [14] I want you to build an ark. Build it out of cypress wood. Make rooms in the ark, and cover it inside and outside with tar. [15] Here's how you will do it: build the ark 450 feet long, 75 feet wide, and 45 feet high. [16] Put a roof[b] on the ark and leave a gap of 18 inches below the roofline *for air to circulate.* Put the door of the ark in its side, and build it with lower, middle, and upper decks. [17] Look! I am going to unleash a torrent and flood the earth to destroy all flesh under the heavens which breathes the breath of life. Everything that is on the earth will die.

[18] But I will make *a pact* with you, *Noah*—a covenant agreement. *To survive, you and your family*—you, your wife, your sons, and your sons' wives—must go into the ark. [19] And, out of all the living creatures *I have made,* you must bring two of each kind into the ark with you, to keep them alive. Bring one male and one female *of each kind.*

[20] Bring all kinds of birds, all sorts of animals, and all varieties of creatures that creep on the ground in pairs, so that each species will survive. [21] Also, you must bring food with you. Bring every kind of food that may be eaten, and store it all *inside the ark.* That way, you and all of the creatures will have *enough* food to eat.

[22] So Noah listened to God, *and he built the ark.* He did everything God asked him to do.

ANALYSIS QUESTIONS

1. What is God's purpose for the ark based on the process he outlined for Noah?

2. What size and shape should the ark be, and what materials should be used to build it?

3. What will Noah do with the ark when he has finished building it?

4. What questions might Noah have that are not answered by the instructions?

Equally detailed instructions on how to follow a carefully prescribed process are given in 2 Chronicles 2 when Solomon sets out to build the temple, but process instructions are not limited to merely outlining how to do something. The technique is employed in Revelation 21:9-27 in reference to "the Bride, the wife of the Lamb" (Rev. 21:9) depicted as "the holy city Jerusalem coming down out of heaven from God" (Rev. 21:10).

THE SCIENTIFIC METHOD[10]

Process is most obvious in scientific pursuits. Francis Bacon (1561-1626) developed the Scientific Method, a process for doing research and verifying a hypothesis by following six logical steps:

1. Observation: Learning about any event noted through the senses.
   a. must be documented scientifically
   b. must be repeatable under similar conditions
   c. must be objective (factual)
2. Problem: A question asked about an observation.

---

[10] See Chapter 11 for a discussion of the Scientific Method as a form of inductive logic.

a. must contain only one unknown

b. must use testable question words that point to a concrete answer

3. Hypothesis: One possible answer to the problem question.

   a. must answer question in a testable fashion

   b. must be limited to one established factor

   c. must include a reason

   d. usually requires research in order to make an "educated" guess

4. Experiment: A test designed to prove or disprove the hypothesis.

   a. must be controlled

   b. must have only one variable

   c. must collect measurable data or information

5. Data Analysis: Data collected must be interpreted based on the hypothesis.

   a. raw data must be organized into a readable form (charts, graphs, etc.)

   b. data must show the relationship between the experiment and the question

6. Conclusion: A Statement that compares the hypothesis to the data.

   a. must use data to state the correctness of the hypothesis, which will turn out to be right or wrong

b. If the hypothesis is correct, it should be able to be replicated to validate results

c. If the hypothesis is incorrect or unanswered, then

    i. the experiment must be re-designed, or

    ii. the question or hypothesis must be restated.

DISCOURSE COMMUNITIES

Process papers launch researchers into the technical jargon of the discourse community in which they work. Theologians have their own language set. So do psychologists, computer programmers, biologists, auto mechanics, physicians, and hundreds of other discourse communities. Such individuals are permitted to write in the first person plural ("we" and "our") when they speak for a clearly defined group of specialists. A letter from an undergraduate physics major illustrates permitted usage when writing about a process:

One theory states that in the nucleus of Helium-3 and He-4, the two protons might be combined in a pre-existing delta particle with +2 charge. We know Δ particles exist, but they're hard to find in the nucleus because first they must be gotten OUT of the nucleus, and once outside they tend to decay into two protons.

The experiment was carried out at the Los Alamos National Laboratory Neutron Science Center (LANSCE). LANSCE houses a proton beam in the Linear Accelerator (LINAC) in which the p+s are accelerated to a significant fraction of the speed of light (186,282.4 miles per second). They then collide with a tungsten spallation target, which ejects neutrons and protons.

The facility provides several collimators for multiple neutron beam paths for different research groups. We use Building 34 to set up a pressurized tank of either He-3 or He-4 with plastic scintillators coupled with photomultiplier tubes at 45° angles to the neutron beam and on the other side of the He target tank. Based on the energies of the protons, we determine if at least some of the protons decayed from Δ++. (Runyon)

ISAAC NEWTON (1642-1727)

Sixteen years after Francis Bacon died, Isaac Newton was born. He put the Scientific Method to excellent use. Famous for identifying the universal law of gravity, he also invented machines, made discoveries in optics and mathematics, designed the first reflecting telescope, and revolutionized the study of mechanics and physics. Newton's letter to the Royal Society concerning his theory about light and colors illustrates how describing a process enhances the reader's understanding, and if it is well done, the reader can replicate the process:

In the beginning of the year 1666 (at which time I applied myself to the grinding of optic glasses of other figures than spherical) I procured me a triangular glass prism to try therewith the celebrated phenomena of colors. And in order thereto having darkened my chamber and made a small hole in my window-shuts to let in a convenient quantity of the sun's light, I placed my prism at his entrance that it might be thereby refracted to the opposite wall. It was at first a very pleasing divertissement to view the vivid and intense colors produced thereby; but after a while, applying myself to consider them more circumspectly, I became surprised to see them in an *oblong* form, which according to the received laws of refraction I expected should have been *circular*. (2156)

The full process Newton followed with this experiment takes many pages to complete, but this sample paragraph illustrates the value to a student in almost any discipline of cultivating the ability to write a process paper.

THE LORAX

Process is not limited to giving instructions or explaining scientific concepts. It is also used in prose and poetry, fact and fiction—whenever an author wishes to provide information in chronological order. Many short stories are fundamentally process papers that incorporate narrative and descriptive writing. A few excerpts from *The Lorax* by Theodor Seuss Geisel illustrate this point. Phrases that are primarily process in nature are underlined:

Way back in the days when the grass was still green and the pond was still wet and the clouds were still clean, and the song of the Swomee-Swans rang out in space. . . .

one morning, I came to this glorious place.

And I first saw the trees! The Truffula Trees!

. . . Mile after mile in the fresh morning breeze. . . .

I felt a great leaping of joy in my heart.

I knew just what I'd do! I unloaded my cart.

In no time at all, I had built a small shop.

Then I chopped down a Truffula Tree with one chop.

And with great skillful skill and with great speedy

speed, <u>I took the soft tuft. And I knitted a thneed</u>!

Now he gets lectured by the Lorax for his environmental

abuse, but just as the Lorax says, "Sir! You are crazy

with greed. There is no one on earth who would buy that

fool Thneed," he manages to sell one and then hatches a

plan to make more:

<u>I rushed 'cross the room,</u> and in no time at all, built a

radio-phone. <u>*I put in a quick call*</u>. I called all my

brothers and uncles and aunts and I said, "Listen

here! Here's a wonderful chance for the whole Once-

ler Family to get mighty rich! Get over here fast!

<u>Take the road to North Nitch. Turn left at</u>

<u>Weehawken. Sharp right at South Stitch</u>."

… Now, chopping one tree at a time was too slow.

<u>So I quickly invented my Super-Axe-Hacker</u>

which whacked off four Truffula Trees at one

smacker. We were making Thneeds four times as fast

as before. . . .

<u>I biggered my factory. I biggered my roads.</u>

<u>I biggered my wagons. I biggered the loads</u>

of the thneeds I shipped out. . . .

"What's *more*," snapped the Lorax. (His dander was

up.) "Let me say a few words about Gluppity-Glupp.

<u>Your machinery chugs on, day and night without stop</u>

<u>Making Gluppity-Glupp. Also Schloppity-Schlopp</u>. And what do you do with this leftover goo?

. . ."<u>You're glumping the pond where the Humming-Fish hummed</u>! No more can they hum, for their gills are all gummed. So I'm sending them off. Oh, their future is dreary."

[Earlier printings add, "I hear things are just as bad up in Lake Erie."]

WRITING ASSIGNMENT

The first step in creating a process paper is to imagine the possible processes common in your discipline, followed by research into what has already been done by specialists in the given field of study. You can then write a paper analyzing a process already carried out by others, or you can create your own process based on models provided by others.

1. Identify your topic here—some aspect of the same topic as your narrative and description papers:

---

2. Write a page of notes to yourself <u>identifying a process</u> integral to your topic. As you brainstorm the potential intricacies, don't just write, "The artist must stretch her canvas and mix her paints

86

before creating an oil painting." That is a little too obvious. A better approach is to identify the process by which she knows how to create a palette of visual effects by mixing primary colors.

3. Now that you have brainstormed a process appropriate to your discourse community, do research to find out the processes explained by specialists in your field of study. These usually appear in scholarly journals and can be located using the following steps on a computer at your college or university library:

A: Select a database provided by your university library. Find an article in a professional journal on your topic and save it on your computer or print appropriate pages for future reference.

B: **Paraphrase, summarize, and quote** material from this source just as you did in the **literature reviews** as explained in Chapters 1 and 2. If you cite an electronic full-text article, MLA requires that the citation include the elements shown in the example below (see *MLA Handbook* 181-184):

Wise, Charles R. "Organizing for Homeland Security." Public Administration Review 62 (2002): 131-144. WilsonSelectPlus [specific database]. FirstSearch

[database provider]. SAU Library [library name].
Web. 25 Feb. 2015 [date viewed/printed].

C: Write the process paper on computer with correct documentation and formatting.

PEER REVIEW: A fellow student should read and evaluate the process paper. The instructor is likely to assign partners for students who have just done the same exercise.

_____ Evaluate the point of view. Is it appropriate for the process being analyzed? It must be written from the third-person point of view unless the author represents a discourse community. In this case, first person plural may be used: ("We discovered," "Our research indicates").

Note: *Implied* second person may be used if instructions are being given, as in "set the temperature at 360," "pour the mixture slowly into the beaker."

Pick one: a. _____ The audience is someone who
                                will perform the process.

              b. _____ The audience will merely
                                understand the process.

_____ Make sure the writer has used clear and unambiguous language so the reader will not encounter unnecessary frustration and inconvenience.

_____ Confirm that all requirements such as time and supplies needed are clearly indicated.

_____ Evaluate the effectiveness of warnings to readers about any possible harm in carrying out this process.

_____ Make sure instructions or steps are given in a logical and appropriate order. If necessary, suggest a revised structure and move paragraphs as needed.

_____ Confirm that each paragraph has only one central idea.

_____ Delete any unnecessary details.

_____ Be sure that the connections between sentences and paragraphs are effective.

_____ Make sure the Works Cited are formatted accurately based on section 5.6 of the _MLA Handbook._

_____ List any questions the author has failed to answer.

PLANNING THE REWRITE

In addition to carefully considering the suggestions of the peer reviewer, review the _MLA Handbook_ 3.1-3.8 "The Mechanics of Writing" and 1.9 "Writing Drafts" for helpful rewriting suggestions. Rewrite the process paper into a logical, smooth-flowing set of instructions that anyone who knows the language of your discourse community can follow.

Thought to ponder: This chapter is itself a process paper from a discourse community explaining how to write a paper in acceptable MLA format. Write a list of the new vocabulary words you have gained from your exposure to this process:

_____

_____

_____

_____

CHAPTER 4: DEFINITION

Narrative tells a story, description adds interest, and process explains how a thing is done. A fourth form of academic writing involves **definition.** *Simple* definitions appear in dictionaries and can be formulated at very primitive levels. "Sterile" can mean "infertile, barren, incapable of producing offspring," or "mentally or spiritually barren," or "free from micro-organisms, aseptic" (OED).

Simple definitions provide a starting point for extended definitions. For example, the dictionary defines "love" as "that state of feeling with regard to a person which manifests itself in concern for the person's welfare" (OED). But even children can quickly get beyond that when asked what love means. Karl, age five, put it in the dating context: "Love is when a girl puts on perfume and a boy puts on shaving cologne and they go out and smell each other." Noelle said, "Love is when you tell a guy you like his shirt—then he wears it every day." Karen added, "When you love somebody, your eyelashes go up and down and little stars come out of you."

More theologically sophisticated children observed, "Love is what's in the room with you at Christmas if you stop opening presents and listen." Nikka, age six, suggested, "If you want to learn to love better, you should start with a friend who you hate." Jessica advised, "You shouldn't say, 'I love you,' unless you mean it. But if you mean it, say it a lot. People forget."

Other youngsters used illustrations to explain love. Rebecca, age eight, said, "When my grandmother got arthritis, she couldn't bend over and paint her toenails, so my grandfather does it for her, even when his hands got arthritis, too. That's Love." Billy, age four, said it this way: "When someone loves you, the way they say your name is different. You just know that your name is safe in their mouth." Four-year-old Lauren said, "I know my older sister loves me because she gives me all her old clothes and has to go out and buy new ones."

The above comments by children are extensions on the definition of love. **Extended definitions** explain an abstract concept in more detail to give readers sophisticated insight. Consider the word "ecclesiology," a Greek-derived word referring to the Church. A book exploring the meaning of this term argues that while "The Council of Nicea declared that the church is *one, holy, catholic*, and *apostolic*," the New Testament reveals that "it would be more biblically accurate to say that the church is:

DIVERSE as well as ONE

CHARISMATIC as well as HOLY

LOCAL as well as CATHOLIC or UNIVERSAL

PROPHETIC as well as APOSTOLIC."

(Snyder and Runyon 17, 22)

These authors wrote an entire book to help define for Christians a more accurate understanding of "ecclesiology." College students in every discipline should begin reading such publications as they learn the language of their discourse community and write their own extended definitions.

DEFINITION READING

The Apostle Paul's famous "love" chapter in his letter to the Corinthians is an extended definition. Corinth at the time of his writing was the "love" capital of the world. This trading city located on the isthmus between the Aegean and Ionian seas teamed with people who equated love with sex thanks to the temple of Poseidon, a place "given over to the worship of the Corinthian Aphrodite (probably a counterpart of the Syrian Astarte) whose temple on the Acrocorinth had more than 1,000 *hierodouloi* (female prostitutes)"

(Gaebelein 176). Paul introduces a new definition of love that would have astounded the Corinthian audience:

What if I speak in the *most elegant* languages of people or in the *exotic* languages of the heavenly messengers, but I live without love? Well then, anything I say is like the clanging of brass or a crashing cymbal.

² What if I have the gift of prophecy, am blessed with knowledge and insight to all the mysteries, or what if my faith is strong enough to scoop a mountain *from its bedrock*, yet I live without love? If so, I am nothing.

³ I could give all that I have to feed the poor, I could surrender my body to be burned *as a martyr*, but if I do not live in love, I gain nothing *by my selfless acts*.

⁴ Love is patient; love is kind. Love isn't envious, doesn't boast, *brag, or strut about.* There's no arrogance in love; ⁵ it's never rude, crude, or indecent—it's not self-absorbed. Love isn't easily upset. Love doesn't tally wrongs ⁶ or celebrate injustice; but truth—*yes, truth*—is love's delight! ⁷ Love puts up with anything and

everything that comes along; it trusts, hopes, and endures no matter what.

[8] Love will never become obsolete. Now as for the prophetic gifts, they will not last; unknown languages will become silent, and the gift of knowledge will no longer be needed. [9] Gifts of knowledge and prophecy are partial at best, *at least for now,* [10] but when the perfection *and fullness of God's kingdom* arrive, all the parts will end.

[11] When I was a child, I spoke, thought, and reasoned in childlike ways *as we all do.* But when I became a man, I left my childish ways behind. [12] For now, we can only see a dim and blurry picture of things, as when we stare into polished metal. I realize that everything I know is only part of the big picture. But one day, *when Jesus arrives,* we will see clearly, face-to-face. In that day, I will fully know just as I have been wholly known *by God.*

[13] But now faith, hope, and love remain; these three *virtues must characterize our lives.* The greatest of these is love. (1 Cor. 13)

ANALYSIS QUESTIONS

1. Make a list of the synonyms Paul used to make his new definition of love more easily understood. (A synonym is an equivalent word, or a word or phrase having the same general sense as another word in the same language.)

2. Distinguish between the "simple" definitions and the "extended" definitions in this essay.

3. Write a paragraph about any new insights you gained about the topic of "love" from having read this definition.

WRITING ASSIGNMENT

Now it is time to write an extended definition. Begin by recognizing that entire books have been written to define a word or concept. Locate a book specific to the topic you are writing about for your extended definition paper. **Hint:** The bibliographies or Works Cited pages of publications consulted for earlier papers are a good place to begin.

1. When you find a book, look in the table of contents for a section closely related to your area of interest.

2. Write a literature review on that section (see guidelines in chapters one and two). Your literature

review should summarize, paraphrase, and quote as necessary to capture the essence of the section.

3. Identify an important word the author uses to tie the section together. For example, the word "definition" is the key term in this chapter of *Integrated Reading and Writing*.

4. Look up the simple definition of that term in a dictionary and write it down.

5. Write an extended definition of that term in your own words based on what you learned from reading the book section.

6. Look at pages 214-219 of the *MLA Handbook* to find out what information to put in a parenthetical reference to identify the above source.

7. Look at pages 129-135 of your *MLA Handbook* to find out what information to put in a Works Cited to accompany the material from the above book, and write it down in the correct format.

   Source one: _____

8. Follow this same format for additional sources.

   Source two: _____

   Source three: _____

9. List all sources in your Works Cited page in alphabetical order, and format each source according to guidelines given in the *MLA Handbook* (129-212).

PEER REVIEW

Have a fellow student read and evaluate the extended definition paper. The instructor is likely to assign partners for students who have just done the same exercise.

1. Read the introduction paragraph and the conclusion paragraph. Edit as necessary so they would belong together if the rest of the paper were missing.

2. Cross out all first person (I, me, my, we, us, our) and all second person (you, your) words to help the author convert the entire manuscript to third person.

3. Consider these questions:

_____ Are the purpose and audience clear and appropriate?

_____ Does the paper avoid the common pitfalls of overly broad, or overly narrow definition?

_____ Are the methods of development suitable for the topic?

_____ Is the paper organized effectively? That is, does it flow logically and answer questions in the order the reader is likely to ask them?

_____ Identify the most boring part and make suggestions on how to make it more interesting.

_____ Review for accuracy the MLA format, punctuation and grammar, and parenthetical references and Works Cited.

_____ Read aloud the portions of the definition that immediately precede and follow source material that is summarized, paraphrased, or quoted. (Parenthetical documentation should follow every instance.) Correct the writing style as necessary so the researched material flows smoothly with the author's voice.

_____ Make suggestions on how the researched material can be more fully integrated into the paper in a way that reflects the author's analysis and synthesis of the research.

PLANNING THE REWRITE

Carefully consider the suggestions of the peer reviewer as you rewrite the extended definition in such a logical and clear way that a person previously unfamiliar with the term being defined will understand. Also, be certain that the format and structure of all parenthetical references and Works Cited entries are precisely correct according to the _MLA Handbook._ Finally, be absolutely certain that your extended definition in no way plagiarizes the original sources. Instructions on how to avoid plagiarism are provided in the _MLA Handbook._

PLAGIARISM QUIZ

Find the answers to the questions below on pages 51-61 of the *MLA Handbook*.

T   F

1. ____ ____ *Plagiarism* derives from the Greek word *plagias* ("plate thief").

2. ____ ____ Unacknowledged use of ideas, information, or expressions is intellectual theft.

3. ____ ____ Passing off another person's material as your own constitutes fraud.

4. ____ ____ Copyright rules limit plagiarism to a legal offense with no ethical implications.

5. ____ ____ Plagiarists easily recover the trust of those they try to deceive.

6. ____ ____ Careful documentation tends to discourage the circulation of error.

7. ____ ____ Plagiarism is impossible to avoid when using electronic or web publications.

8. ____ ____ Because research has the power to affect opinions and actions, responsible writers compose their work with great care, often spending as much time documenting sources as writing original material.

Multiple Choice

9. Regarding unintentional plagiarism, the *MLA Handbook* suggests that writers should keep careful notes on

   a. their ideas

   b. their summaries and paraphrases of the ideas and facts of others

   c. exact wording copied from sources

   d. all of the above

   e. none of the above

10. Documentation is not needed in the following instances. (Circle all that apply.)

    a. When quoting familiar proverbs or well-known quotations.

    b. When writing statements of common knowledge.

    c. When quoting the Bible or other well-known religious documents.

    d. When quoting daily newspapers or websites with no print equivalent.

    e. When quoting information obtained by personal interviews or survey research.

The importance of avoiding plagiarism cannot be overstated. Some university professors (including the author of this text) automatically fail any student caught plagiarizing, and many educational institutions publish their own plagiarism guidelines which they expect students to know and follow. For more information, an internet search on "plagiarism" will turn up numerous sources and guidelines for learning how to avoid plagiarism.

CHAPTER 5: ILLUSTRATION

All the forms of writing covered so far in this text, narrative, description, process, and definition can be improved with **illustrations.** Some definitions of love in the last chapter used illustrations, which can be as brief as a few words or as long as a chapter. When five-year-old Karl tried to define love he actually illustrated it: "Love is when a girl puts on perfume and a boy puts on shaving cologne and they go out and smell each other."

Illustration is the art of comparing a new concept with something already familiar to the reader, and illustrations are chosen based on the audience. A psychologist talking to a computer technician illustrates his point successfully when he says that the brain stores information "like a silicon chip." The same message needs to be illustrated differently to children in the African bush where there is no electricity or computers. Perhaps the psychologist will make some reference to an elephant if he is aware of the saying in Africa that "elephants never forget."

In literature, culturally relevant symbols are often used to convey meaning. The symbol often dictates the interpretation. A father who learns to tell time with an analogue watch might envision time as passing in a "clock-wise" direction—in a circle to the right. He may extrapolate from this image of minutes and hours a mental picture of the calendar as a circle with March in the three o'clock position, June at six o'clock, September at nine o'clock, and the break between December and January at precisely midnight. If this man's son learns to tell time via a digital watch and therefore envisions days, months, and years as lined up in linear fashion from left to right, he represents a paradigm shift—the two types of clocks have become opposing symbols that influence the way time is perceived. Due to this shift, the son may not understand his father's "clockwise" symbol.

Illustration is a high art. It must always serve the larger context. The risk is that the illustration will overtake the message. Many a pastor has thought he preached on "The Consequences of Disobedience" when most people in attendance missed his point and thought he just told a story about a big fish that swallowed Jonah. Successful illustrations clarify the point or help readers understand a concept in deeper ways.

ILLUSTRATION READINGS

When the reader has no possible reference point for understanding the thing being taught, an illustration may be the only way to explain a concept. God has this problem—without revelation, earth-bound humankind has no way to comprehend heaven-grounded truth. Therefore, it is no surprise that the Bible provides some of the finest readings that model the art of illustration. Three selections are provided below.

James 2

My brothers and sisters, *I know you've heard this before, but* stop playing favorites! Do not try to blend the genuine faith of our glorious Lord Jesus, the Anointed One, *with your silly pretentiousness.* [2] If an affluent gentleman enters your gathering wearing the finest clothes and priceless jewelry, *don't trip over each other trying to welcome him.* And if a penniless bum crawls in with his shabby clothes *and a stench fills the room, don't look away or pretend you didn't notice—offer him a seat up front, next to you.* [3-4] If you tell the wealthy man, "Come sit by me; there's plenty of room," but tell the vagrant, "Oh, these seats are saved. Go over there," then you'll be judging *God's children* out of evil motives.

[5] My dear brothers and sisters, listen: God has picked the poor of this world to become *unfathomably* rich in faith and ultimately to inherit the Kingdom, which He has pledged to those who love Him. [6] *By favoring the rich,* you have mocked the poor. *And, correct me if I'm wrong,* but isn't it the rich who step on you while climbing the ladder of success? And isn't it the rich who *take advantage of you and* drag you into court? [7] Aren't they the ones mocking the noble name *of our God,* the One calling us?

[8] *Remember His call, and* live by the royal law found in Scripture*:* love others as you love yourself. You'll be doing very well if you can get this down. [9] But if you show favoritism—*paying attention to those who can help you in some way, while ignoring those who seem to need all the help*—you'll be sinning and condemned by the law. [10] For if a person could keep all of the laws and yet break just one; it would be like breaking them all. [11] The same God who said, "Do not commit adultery," also says, "Do not murder." If you break either of these commands, you're a lawbreaker, *no matter how you look at it.* [12] So live your life in such a way that acknowledges that one day you will be judged. But the law that

judges also gives freedom, [13] although you can't expect to be shown mercy if you refuse to show mercy. *But hear this:* mercy always wins against judgment! *Thank God!*

[14] Brothers and sisters, it doesn't make any sense to say you have faith and act in a way that denies that faith. *Mere talk never gets you very far, and* a commitment to Jesus only in words will not save you. [15] It would be like seeing a brother or sister without any clothes *out in the cold* and begging for food, and [16] saying, "Shalom, *friend,* you should get inside where it's warm and eat something," but doing nothing about his needs—*leaving him cold and alone on the street.* What good would your words alone do? [17] The same is true with faith. Without actions, *faith is useless. By itself,* it's *as good as* dead. [18] I know what you're thinking: "OK, you have faith. And I have actions. Now let's see your faith without works, and I'll show you a faith that works."

[19] Do you think that just believing there's one God is going to get you anywhere? The demons believe that, too, and it terrifies them! [20] *The fact is,* faith has to show itself through works performed in faith. If you don't recognize that, then you're an empty soul. [21] Wasn't our father Abraham made right

with God by laying his son Isaac on the altar? [22] The faith *in his heart* was made known in his behavior. In fact, his commitment was perfected by his obedience. [23] That's what Scripture means when it says, "Abraham entrusted himself to God, and God credited him with righteousness." *And living a faithful life* earned Abraham the title of "God's friend." [24] *Just like our father in the faith,* we are made right with God through good works, not simply by what we believe or think. [25] Even Rahab the prostitute was made right with God by hiding the spies and aiding in their escape. [26] Removing action from faith is like removing breath from a body. All you have left is a corpse.

ANALYSIS QUESTIONS

1. List all of the examples used by the author to illustrate his point.

2. How does each example make the above comments by James more interesting and easy to understand?

I Corinthians 12

Now let me turn to *some issues about* spiritual gifts, brothers and sisters. There's much you need to learn.

[2] Remember *the way you used to live* when you were pagans *apart from God*? You were engrossed—enchanted with voiceless idols, led astray *by mere images carved by human hands.* [3] With that in mind, I want you to understand that no one saying "Jesus is cursed" is operating under God's Spirit, and no one confessing "Jesus is Lord" can do so without the Holy Spirit's inspiration.

[4] Now there are many kinds of *grace* gifts, but they are all from the same Spirit. [5] There are many different ways to serve, but *they're all directed by* the same Lord. [6] There are many amazing working gifts in the church, but it is the same God who energizes them all in all *who have the gifts.*

[7] Each believer has received a gift that manifests the Spirit's *power and presence*. That gift is given for the good of the whole community. [8] The Spirit gives one person a word of wisdom, but to the next person the same Spirit gives a word of knowledge. [9] Another will receive *the gift of* faith by the same Spirit, and still another gifts of healing—all from the one Spirit. [10] One person is enabled *by the Spirit* to perform miracles, another to prophesy, while another is enabled to distinguish *those prophetic* spirits. The next one speaks in various kinds of unknown languages, while another is able to interpret those languages. [11] One Spirit works all these things in each of them individually as He sees fit.

[12] Just as a body is one whole made up of many different parts, and all the different parts comprise the one body, so it is with the Anointed One. [13] We were all ceremonially washed through baptism together into one body by one Spirit. *No matter our heritage*—Jew or Greek, insider or outsider—*no matter our status*—oppressed or free—we were all given the one Spirit to drink. [14] *Here's what I mean:* the body is not made of one large part but of many *different parts*. [15] Would it seem right for the foot to cry, "I am not a hand, so I couldn't be part of this

body"? Even if it did, it wouldn't be any less joined to the body. [16] And what about an ear? If an ear started to whine, "I am not an eye; I shouldn't be attached to this body," in all its pouting, it is still part of the body. [17] Imagine the entire body as an eye. How would a giant eye be able to hear? And if the entire body were an ear, how would an ear be able to smell?

[18] *This is where God comes in.* God has meticulously put this body together; He placed each part in the exact place to perform the exact function He wanted. [19] If all members were a single part, where would the body be? [20] So now, many members *function* within the one body. [21] The eye cannot wail at the hand, "I have no need for you," nor could the head bellow at the feet, "I won't go one more step with you." [22] It's actually the opposite. The members who seem to have the weaker functions are necessary to keep the body moving; [23] the body parts that seem less important we treat as some of the most valuable; and those unfit, untamed, unpresentable members we treat with an even greater modesty. [24] That's something the more presentable members don't need. But God designed the body in such a way that greater significance is given to the *seemingly* insignificant

part. [25] That way there should be no division in the body; instead, all the parts mutually depend on and care for one another. [26] If one part is suffering, then all the members suffer alongside it. If one member is honored, then all the members celebrate alongside it.

[27] You are the body of the Anointed, *the Liberating King;* each and every one of you is a *vital* member. [28] God has appointed *gifts* in the assembly: first emissaries, second prophets, third teachers, then miracle workers, healers, helpers, administrators, and then those who speak with various unknown languages. [29] Are all members gifted as emissaries? Are all gifted with prophetic utterance? Are all teachers? Do all work miracles? [30] Or are all gifted in healing arts? Do all speak or interpret unknown languages? *Of course not.* [31] Pursue the greater gifts, and let me tell you of a more excellent way—love.

ANALYSIS QUESTIONS

3. Metaphors are a type of illustration. (See Chapter 2 for more information on metaphors.) How does the extended metaphor of the "Body" help the reader comprehend the author's meaning?

4. Describe the images that jump into your mind as you read about the "body" metaphor.

5. Try to think of another metaphor that could illustrate the same truth to a modern reader. Is your metaphor better than Paul's? Why or why not?

6. How does the author's sense of humor contribute to make the passage more interesting and enjoyable to read?

Matthew 20: 1-16

Jesus: The kingdom of heaven is like a wealthy landowner who got up early in the morning and went out, first thing, to hire workers to tend his vineyard. [2] He agreed to pay them a day's wage for the day's work. The workers headed to the vineyard *while the landowner headed home to deal with some paperwork.* [3] About three hours later, he went back to the marketplace. He saw *some unemployed* men standing around with nothing to do.

Landowner: [4] *Do you need some work?* Go over to my vineyard *and join the crew there.* I'll pay you well.

So off they went *to join the crew at the vineyard.* [5] About three hours later, and then three hours after that, *the landowner went back to the market and saw another crew of men and hired them, too, sending them off to his vineyard and promising to pay them well.* [6] Then finally late in the afternoon, *at the cusp of night,* the landowner walked again through *the marketplace,* and he saw other *workers* still standing around.

Landowner: Why have you been standing here all day, doing nothing?

Workers: [7] Because no one has hired us.

Landowner: Well, you should go over to my vineyard *and work.*

And off the workers went. [8] When quitting time arrived, the landowner called to his foreman.

Landowner: Pay the workers their day's wages, beginning with the workers I hired most recently and ending with the workers who have been here all day.

[9] So the workers who had been hired just a short while before came to the foreman, and he paid them each a day's wage. [10] *Then other workers who had*

arrived during the day were paid, each of them a day's wage. Finally, the workers who'd been toiling since early morning came thinking they'd be paid more, but the foreman paid each of them a day's wage. [11] As they received their pay, this last group of workers began to protest.

First Workers: [12] *We've been here since the crack of dawn!* And you're paying us the exact same wage you paid the crew that just showed up. *We deserve more than they do.* We've been slogging in the heat of the sun all day—*these others haven't worked nearly as long as we have!*

[13] *The landowner heard these protests.*

Landowner *(to a worker)*: Friend, no one has been wronged here today. *This isn't about what you deserve.* You agreed to work for a day's wage, did you not? [14] So take your money and go home. *I can give my money to whomever I please, and* it pleases me to pay everyone the same amount of money. [15] Do you think I don't have the right to dispose of my money as I wish? Or does my generosity somehow prick at you?

[16] *And that is your picture:* The last will be first and the first will be last.

ANALYSIS QUESTIONS

7. Jesus was a master at telling stories to illustrate difficult concepts. What do you understand about heaven now that was not clear to you before reading this?

8. How did the illustrations of Jesus help you gain these new insights?

9. What have you learned from this story about God's point of view?

WRITING ASSIGNMENT

Review all the material you have written: narrative, description, process, and definition. How can this material be improved by illustration? Most likely the definition paper will be the one that can be most dramatically improved, because it is difficult to define an abstract concept without illustrating it. Research will be necessary as you search for accurately chosen illustrations to expand your paper. This means you will write at least one new literature review and a new source to your growing collection of Works Cited.

In addition to researching the perfect illustration, your own illustrations can also be added. They can be as brief as prepositional phrases (instead of just "angry" you might write, "angry <u>as a rabid dog</u>" to show the intensity of the anger) or as long as a parable of Jesus, all depending on what is needed to convey the intended meaning.

Finally, not all illustrations are narratives. Academic writing often uses **tables, figures,** and **examples**. All such illustrations should be inserted in the manuscript in the most logical and convenient place for the reader and documented as prescribed in the *MLA Handbook* (see pages 118-121). Make a list here of the ideas for illustration that immediately come to mind:

_____

_____

_____

_____

_____

Write one page worth of illustration and insert it in the appropriate places in previously written materials. Highlight the added illustrative text and bring the full manuscript to class for a peer review. Since academic writing is usually produced on a black and white printer, avoid color highlights. Instead, follow the example here using the 25% gray highlight selected from the toolbar in Microsoft Word.

PEER REVIEW

Have a fellow student read and evaluate the illustrations added to previously written material. The instructor is likely to assign partners for students who have done the same exercise. Evaluate each illustration as follows:

_____ Does the illustration illuminate the idea without introducing irrelevant material?

_____ Is the illustration interesting?

_____ Are an appropriate number of examples used?

_____ Is the paper organized effectively with illustrations in the right places? If not, suggest where illustrations might be moved for better effect.

_____ Identify the most boring part of this paper and delete it or make suggestions on how to make it more interesting.

_____ Identify the most interesting part of this paper and tell the author why it is interesting.

_____ Review for accuracy the formatting of the Works Cited.

_____ Review for accuracy the formatting of the tables and figures, and examples (see *MLA Handbook* 118-121).

_____ Cross out all first person singular (I, me, my, mine) and all second person (you, your) words to help the author achieve an appropriately objective paper.

Write a brief evaluation of the ways this paper is more effective now that it has been illustrated:

_____

_____

_____

_____

_____

_____

PLANNING THE REWRITE

Rewrite the illustration using the guidelines provided in the peer review. As you think about your illustrations, also contemplate the choice of words and the images used. A common mistake is to project the current meaning of a symbol backward onto past literature and therefore miss the intended meaning. For example, "gay" once meant "happy" in reference to attitude and "colorful" in reference to clothing. Make word choices that accurately communicate your intended meaning to the reader.

A second common mistake is to presume that the illustration accomplishes more than it actually does.

Northrop Frye illustrates what is meant here in his observations regarding Samson in the Book of Judges:

> We may notice that Samson's name resembles early Semitic words for the sun, and that his story tells of a supernaturally powerful hero associated with the burning of crops, who eventually falls into a dark prison-house in the west. That the story shows structural or narrative analogies to the kind of story that might be suggested by the passage of the sun across the sky is true, and no storyteller worth his keep would try to eliminate such analogies. But to say that the Samson stories "derive from" a solar myth or that a solar myth "lies behind" them is to say more than anyone knows. (*Great Code* 35)

Review your illustrations to assure that you have made accurate word choices and realistic applications of images and ideas. Do not over state your case. In so doing you will gain credibility by avoiding the pitfall of saying more than anyone truly knows about the topic.

CHAPTER 6: CLASSIFICATION

Narrative tells a story, description stimulates the five senses, process shows how a thing is done, extended definitions explain aspects of a discipline, and all of them are more effective if well illustrated. **Classification** is yet another useful skill. To classify means to put with others of the same type, to "pigeon-hole," to create a category for organizing ideas. When advertisements are put into categories they are called "classified ads," and when students are put in classes with others of similar age or ability, they have been classified. The entire network of information available on the web is accessible mainly through an elaborate system of classification.

A world without classification would be pure chaos. How would customers find anything in a grocery store if rugs were piled next to bananas? Classification places things in categories so life can be efficient and logical. Respond to the following questions to see the many ways in which grouping things into categories is fundamental to daily living.

List here the items generally placed in a closet:

_____

_____

List here the items generally placed in a kitchen:

_____

_____

List here the likely reactions if a stranger placed your kitchen items in your closet, or your closet items in your kitchen:

_____

_____

A man in need of a bicycle does not go shopping at an automotive dealership; a woman in need of cooking oil does not visit a furniture store. Make a list of ten important categories you use to make life at home, work, and church more efficient and logical.

1. _____
2. _____
3. _____
4. _____
5. _____
6. _____

7. _____

8. _____

9. _____

10. _____

The *MLA Handbook* models effective classification—it is easy to find the correct format for a Works Cited entry once the structure of the *MLA Handbook* is understood. Using the table of contents (v-xii) and the index (265-292), the college writing student is empowered to accurately document every conceivable source. Similarly, when writers place ideas in categories, they establish intelligent ways of thinking that make communicating the message to their audience efficient and logical.

CLASSIFICATION READINGS

Read the text below and try to identify the classification inherent in Isaiah 28:24-29:

Does a farmer constantly plow and turn the soil to plant his seed? *No, of course not.* When he's leveled *and tilled* the soil, *doesn't he plant each seed according to its specifications?* He scatters the dill, sows the cummin, plants the wheat in rows, puts barley and spelt where they grow best.

God instructs and directs the farmer in how best
to manage the land. For dill isn't threshed with a
sledge, and you don't roll a cart over the cummin.
Dill is properly beaten free with one kind of stick,
  and cummin with another.

Similarly, you have to grind grain *to have flour*
for bread, but you don't grind it endlessly. When the
wheel on the cart and the horses go over the grain,
you must be careful not to crush it.

The Eternal, Commander of *heavenly* armies,
  is the source of such wisdom. His advice is
wonderful.

ANALYSIS QUESTION:

1. Explain how the art of classification was useful to
   Isaiah, and why this passage makes more sense
   because of the classification employed.

The Apostle Paul was a master of classification as
revealed in this passage:[11]

---

[11] Notice two options for documenting biblical
references. The first quote identifies the source (Isaiah 28:24-
29) in the text, so no parenthetical reference is needed. The
second quote from the Apostle Paul uses parenthetical
reference at the end to identify the exact source.

[5] If you live your life animated by the flesh—*namely, your fallen, corrupt nature*—then your mind is focused on the matters of the flesh. But if you live your life animated by the Spirit—*namely, God's indwelling presence*—then your focus is on the work of the Spirit. [6] A mind focused on the flesh is doomed to death, but a mind focused on the Spirit will find full life and complete peace. [7] You see, a mind focused on the flesh is declaring war against God; it defies the authority of God's law and is incapable of following His path. [8] *So it is clear that* God takes no pleasure in those who live oriented to the flesh.

[9] But you do not live in the flesh. You live in the Spirit, assuming, of course, that the Spirit of God lives inside of you. *The truth is that* anyone who does not have the Spirit of the Anointed living within does not belong to God. [10] If the Anointed One lives within you, even though the body is *as good as* dead because of *the effects of* sin, the Spirit is infusing you with life now that you are right with God. [11] If the Spirit of the One who resurrected Jesus from the dead lives inside of you, then *you can be sure that* He who raised Him will cast *the light of* life into your mortal bodies through the life-giving power of the Spirit residing in you.

[12] So, my brothers and sisters, you owe the flesh nothing! You do not need to live according to its ways, *so abandon its oppressive regime.* [13] For if your life is just about satisfying the impulses of your sinful nature, then prepare to die. But if you have invited the Spirit to destroy these selfish desires, you will experience life. [14] If the Spirit of God is leading you, then *take comfort in knowing* you are His children. [15] You see, you have not received a spirit that returns you to slavery, so you have nothing to fear. The Spirit you have received adopts you *and welcomes you* into God's own family. That's why we call out to Him, "Abba! Father!" *as we would address a loving daddy.* [16] *Through that prayer,* God's Spirit confirms in our spirits that we are His children. [17] If we are God's children, that means we are His heirs along with the Anointed, set to inherit everything that is His. If we share His sufferings, *we know that* we will ultimately share in His glory. (Rom. 8:5-17)

ANALYSIS QUESTION

2. Make a list of the categories of classification used by Paul in the above passage.

Similarly, look for classification in a treatise on the supremacy of Jesus:

[15] He is the *exact* image of the invisible God, the firstborn of creation, *the eternal*. [16] It was by Him that everything was created: the heavens, the earth, all things within and upon them, all things seen and unseen, thrones and dominions, *spiritual* powers and authorities. Every detail was crafted through His design, *by His own hands,* and for His purposes. [17] He has always been! *It is His hand* that holds everything together. [18] He is the head of this body, the church. He is the beginning, the first of those to be reborn from the dead, so that *in every aspect, at every view,* in everything—He is first. [19] God was pleased that all His fullness should *forever* dwell in the Son [20] who, *as predetermined by God,* bled peace into the world by His death on the cross as God's means of reconciling to Himself the whole creation—all things in heaven and all things on earth.

[21] You were once at odds *with God,* wicked in your ways and evil in your minds; [22] but now He has

reconciled you in His body—in His flesh through His death—so that He can present you to God holy, blameless, and *totally* free of imperfection [23] as long as you stay planted in the faith. So don't venture away from what you have heard *and taken to heart*: the *living* hope of the good news that has been announced to all creation under heaven and has captured me, Paul, as its servant. (Col.1:15-23)

ANALYSIS QUESTIONS

3. Explain how classification was a useful technique in this treatise on the supremacy of Christ.

4. Discuss how classification is typically done in your discipline. (Musicians may classify information differently than chemists; social scientists may do it differently than mathematicians; theologians may do it differently than artists.)

5. Explain how the classification already done by pioneers in your discipline has made it easier to understand and work within that discipline.

WRITING ASSIGNMENT

Without doing any research, write a paragraph out of your own mind that identifies three important strategies for classification followed in your area of study.

Now go online and search for "classification and _____." Fill in the blank with a word from your discipline. Search the internet links until you find a system for classification that may prove valuable in your education and career. Write a paragraph identifying this source and explaining how it is useful. The information you have just selected will very likely be useful in conjunction with other structures such as when you create a **comparison** essay, the subject of the next chapter.

SECTION II: COLLEGE WRITING ESSAYS

Section 1 of *Integrated Reading and Writing* offered brief readings that modeled various writing techniques. Taken together, these techniques give the writer a set of tools useful in writing essays. Section II provides opportunities to read and experience media events and explore those events by writing comparison and media analysis essays.

CHAPTER 7: COMPARISON

Comparisons show relationships and can be done in either the alternating pattern or the block pattern. The <u>alternating pattern</u> quickly compares two things— sometimes within a single sentence: "The corn field is green whereas the wheat field is golden." A second example: "The tall stalks of corn shimmer as they rustle in the afternoon breeze while the swaying heads of wheat exude a deep luster as they bow under the blazing sun."

The alternating pattern can also devote one sentence to the first thing and another sentence to the second thing: "Pedro has three mules that carry water each morning and evening from the reservoir to the metal tank where grazing sheep conveniently drink within their pen without being threatened by wild dogs. However, his neighbor Pablo has rigged up a pump and hose running from the river to his barn where he gives the pigs their fill of water with the simple twist of a faucet handle." The following poem models how the alternating pattern carries with it an implicit comparison:

Our Love Is Not Donne Yet

Donne said 'tis not the bodies marry, but the minds

But I them both in you angelic find.

He said hope not for mind in women—at best

They just sweetness and wit possess.

But I with you found this plus all the rest.

Said he, lovers dream a rich and long delight

But get a winter-seeming summer's night,

While I with you (what have we done so right?)

Find sun and flowers all through winter's night.

He could not find the hidden mystery

But I have loved, and got, and told,

So as our love will blossom and unfold

I will with you abide as we grow old.

I found a love that's rich, and deep, and true,

A mighty gift from God reached me in you.[12]

In contrast to the above alternating pattern, the writer who describes corn for a full paragraph, then writes about wheat in the next paragraph, has adopted the <u>block pattern</u> of comparison. So has the publisher

---

[12] Daniel V. Runyon, "Our Love Is Not Donne Yet," unpublished poem written for his wife on their wedding anniversary. The author compares his own experience with that described by John Donne in "Love's Alchemy."

who devotes an entire chapter to Pedro's farming technique, followed by a chapter devoted to Pablo's farming technique. Mark Twain uses the block pattern in "Continued Perplexities," *Life on the Mississippi:*

Now when I had mastered the language of this water and had come to know every trifling feature that bordered the great river as familiarly as I knew the letters of the alphabet, I had made a valuable acquisition. But I had lost something, too. I had lost something which could never be restored to me while I lived. All the grace, the beauty, the poetry, had gone out of the majestic river! I still kept in mind a certain wonderful sunset which I witnessed when steamboating was new to me. A broad expanse of the river was turned to blood; in the middle distance the red hue brightened into gold, through which a solitary log came floating, black and conspicuous; in one place a long, slanting mark lay sparkling upon the water; in another the surface was broken by boiling, tumbling rings that were as many-tinted as an opal; where the ruddy flush was faintest was a smooth spot that was covered with graceful circles and radiating lines, ever so delicately traced; the shore on our left was densely wooded, and the somber shadow that fell from this forest was broken in one place by a long, ruffled trail that shone like silver; and high above the forest wall a clean-stemmed dead tree waved a single leafy bough that glowed like a flame in the unobstructed splendor that was flowing from the sun. There were graceful curves, reflected images, woody heights, soft distances, and over the whole scene, far and near, the dissolving lights drifted steadily, enriching it every passing moment with new marvels of coloring.

I stood like one bewitched. I drank it in, in a speechless rapture. The world was new to me and I had never seen anything like this at home. But as I have said, a day came when I began to cease from noting the glories and the charms which the moon and the sun and the twilight wrought upon the river's face; another day came when I ceased altogether to note them. Then, if that sunset scene had been repeated, I should have looked upon it without rapture and should have commented upon it inwardly after this fashion: "This sun means that we are going to have wind tomorrow; that floating log means that the river is rising, small thanks to it; that slanting mark on the water refers to a bluff reef which is going to kill somebody's steamboat one of these nights, if it keeps on stretching out like that; those tumbling 'boils' show a dissolving bar and a changing channel there; the lines and circles in the slick water over yonder are a warning that that troublesome place is shoaling up dangerously; that silver streak in the shadow of the forest is the 'break' from a new snag and he has located himself in the very best place he could have found to fish for steamboats; that tall dead tree, with a single living branch, is not going to last long, and then how is a body ever going to get through this blind place at night without the friendly old landmark?"

No, the romance and beauty were all gone from the river. All the value any feature of it had for me now was the amount of usefulness it could furnish toward compassing the safe piloting of a steamboat. Since those days, I have pitied doctors from my heart. What does the lovely flush in a beauty's cheek mean to a doctor but a "break" that ripples above some deadly disease? Are not all her visible charms sown thick with what are to him the signs and symbols of hidden decay? Does he ever see her beauty at all, or doesn't he simply view her professionally and comment upon her unwholesome condition all to himself? And doesn't he sometimes wonder whether he has gained most or lost most by learning his trade? (64-66)

ANALYSIS QUESTIONS:

1. Write a paragraph speculating on why Twain chose the block pattern of comparison and the extremely long sentence in paragraph one.

2. Twain's seemingly endless sentences create a sense of flow so that the reader feels the steamboat under him and the length of the day and the dream-like qualities of the observations presented. If Twain had used the alternating pattern of comparison, what would be lost?

3. Explain what it would take to convert this portion of Twain's text from the block pattern to the alternating pattern of comparison. What could be gained by using the alternating pattern?

COMPARISON READINGS

The Apostle Paul used the art of comparison when he wrote to the Ephesians to help them understand their own transformed lives. Notice how he skillfully uses the past and present tense to create categories of comparison:

Ephesians 2

As for you, *don't you remember how you used to just exist? Corpses,* dead *in life,* buried by transgressions, [2] wandering the course of this *perverse* world. *You were the offspring* of the prince of the power of air—*oh, how he owned you,* just as he still controls those living in disobedience. *I'm not talking about the outsiders alone;* [3] we were all guilty of falling headlong for the persuasive passions of this world; we all have had our fill of indulging the flesh and mind, *obeying impulses to follow perverse thoughts motivated by dark powers.* As a result, our natural inclinations led us to be children of wrath, just like the rest of humankind.

[4] But God, with the *unfathomable* richness of His love and mercy focused on us, [5] united us with the Anointed One and infused our lifeless souls with life—even though we were buried under mountains of sin—and saved us by His grace. [6] He raised us up with Him and seated us in the heavenly realms with *our beloved* Jesus the Anointed, *the Liberating King.* [7] *He did this for a reason:* so that for all eternity we will stand as a living testimony to the incredible riches of His grace and kindness that He freely gives to us by uniting us with Jesus the Anointed. [8-9] For it's by God's grace that you have been saved. You receive it through faith. It was not *our plan or* our effort. It is God's gift, *pure and simple.* You didn't

earn it, *not one of us did*, so don't go around bragging *that you must have done something amazing.* [10] For we are the product of His hand, *heaven's poetry etched on lives,* created in the Anointed, Jesus, to accomplish the good works God arranged long ago.

[11] So never forget how you used to be. Those of you born as outsiders *to Israel* were *outcasts*, branded "the uncircumcised" by those who bore the sign of the covenant in their flesh, a sign made with human hands. [12] You had absolutely no connection to the Anointed; you were strangers, separated from God's people. You were aliens to the covenant they had with God; you were hopelessly stranded without God in a *fractured* world. [13] But now, because of Jesus the Anointed *and His sacrifice, all of that has changed.* God gathered you who were so far away and brought you near to Him by the *royal* blood of the Anointed, *our Liberating King.*

[14] He is the embodiment of our peace, *sent once and for all* to take down the great barrier of hatred and hostility that has divided us so that we can be one. [15] He offered His body *on the sacrificial altar* to bring an end to the law's ordinances and dictations *that separated Jews from the outside nations. His desire was* to create in His body one new humanity from the

140

two *opposing groups*, thus creating peace.

¹⁶ *Effectively* the cross becomes God's means to kill off the hostility *once and for all* so that He is able to reconcile them both to God in this one new body.

¹⁷ The Great Preacher of peace *and love* came for you, and *His voice* found those of you who were near and those who were far away. ¹⁸ By Him both have access to the Father in one Spirit. ¹⁹ And so you are no longer called outcasts and wanderers but citizens with God's people, *members of God's holy family,* and residents of His household. ²⁰ You are being built on a *solid* foundation: *the message* of the prophets and *the voices* of God's chosen emissaries[a] with Jesus, the Anointed Himself, the *precious* cornerstone. ²¹ The building is joined together *stone by stone—all of us chosen and sealed* in Him, rising up to become a holy temple in the Lord. ²² In Him you are being built together, creating a *sacred* dwelling place *among you* where God can live in the Spirit.

ANALYSIS QUESTION

4. In this comparison the author continually switches back and forth between the past tense ("you were") and the present tense ("but now"). Make two

comprehensive lists organized in two columns. One list should show the situation as identified in the past tense features of Ephesians 2, the other of the present tense features.

Situation in the past	Situation in the present
_____	_____
_____	_____
_____	_____
_____	_____
_____	_____
_____	_____

Ephesians 5

So imitate God. *Follow Him* like adored children, [2] and live in love as the Anointed One loved you—so much that He gave Himself as a fragrant sacrifice, pleasing God.

[3] *Listen,* don't let any kind of immorality be breathed among you. Any demoralizing behaviors (*perverse sexual acts, uncleanliness,* greediness, *and the like*) are inappropriate topics of conversation for those set apart as God's people. [4] Don't swear or spurt nonsense. Don't make harsh jokes *or clown around.* Make proper use of your words, and offer them thankfully in praise. [5] This is what we know for

142

certain: no one who engages in loose sex, impure actions, and greed—which is just a form of idolatry—has any inheritance in the kingdom of God and His Anointed.

[6] Don't be fooled by people whose sentences are compounded with *useless words,* empty words—*they just show they are empty souls.* For, in His wrath, God will judge all the children of disobedience for these kinds *of sins.* [7] So don't *be persuaded into their ignorance*; *and don't* cast your lot with them [8] because, although you were once the personification of darkness, you are now light in the Lord. So act like children of the light. [9] For the fruit of the light is all that is good, right, and true. [10] Make it your aim to learn what pleases our Lord. [11] Don't get involved with the fruitless works of darkness; instead, expose them *to the light of God.* [12] You see, it's a disgrace to speak of their secrets (so don't even talk about what they do when no one is looking). [13-14] When the light shines, it exposes *even the dark and shadowy* things and turns them into *pure reflections of* light. This is why they sing,

> Awake, you sleeper!
> Rise from your grave,
> And the Anointed One will shine on you.

[15] So be careful how you live; *be mindful of your steps*. Don't run around like idiots *as the rest of the world does*. Instead, walk as the wise! [16] Make the most of every *living and breathing* moment because these are evil times. [17] So understand *and be confident in* God's will, and don't live thoughtlessly. [18] Don't drink wine excessively. The drunken path *is a reckless path. It* leads nowhere. Instead, let God fill you with the Holy Spirit. [19] *When you are filled with the Spirit, you are empowered to* speak to each other in *the soulful words of* pious songs, hymns, and spiritual songs; to sing and make music with your hearts attuned to God; [20] and to give thanks to God the Father every day through the name of our Lord Jesus the Anointed for all He has done.

[21] *And the Spirit makes it possible to* submit *humbly* to one another out of respect for the Anointed. [22] Wives, *it should be no different* with your husbands. Submit to them as you do to the Lord, [23] for God has given husbands a *sacred* duty to lead as the Anointed leads the church and serves as the head. (The church is His body; He is her Savior.) [24] So wives should submit to their husbands, *respectfully,* in all things, just as the church yields to the Anointed One.

[25-26] Husbands, you must love your wives so *deeply, purely, and sacrificially that we can understand it only when we* compare it to the love the Anointed One has for *His bride,* the church. *We know* He gave Himself up completely to make her His own, washing her clean of all her impurity with water and *the powerful presence of* His word. [27] *He has given Himself* so that He can present the church as His radiant bride, unstained, unwrinkled, and unblemished—*completely free from all impurity*—holy and innocent before Him. [28] So husbands should care for their wives *as if their lives depended on it,* the same way they care for their own bodies. As you love her, you ultimately are loving *part of* yourself *(remember, you are one flesh).* [29] No one really hates his own body; he takes care to feed and love it, just as the Anointed takes care of His church, [30] because we are *living* members of His body. [31] "And this is the reason a man leaves his father and his mother and is united with his wife; the two come together as one flesh."[a] [32] There is a great mystery *reflected* in this *Scripture,* and I say that it has to do with *the marriage of* the Anointed One and the church.

[33] Nevertheless, each husband is to love *and protect*

his own wife as if she were his very heart, and each wife is to respect her own husband.

ANALYSIS QUESTIONS

5. Write a paragraph explaining how the analogy to death and life make this comparison essay more convincing.

6. What other analogies besides death and life are used in the above texts, and how do they create a sense of comparison that helps the author communicate his message?

7. Write a paragraph explaining the ways in which you agree or disagree with this statement: "Opposites make attractive comparisons."

WRITING ASSIGNMENT

The role of novels in recent centuries has largely been replaced by movies today. Many people have watched more movies than they have read books. Writers must stay in touch with culture by watching these productions as well. Therefore, this assignment invites students to watch a movie and then write a paper in which they compare some aspect of that production with some aspect of their own field of study.

At the superficial level, Anna in *Frozen* could be compared to any other self-realized protagonist in other epic tales or films. But comparisons can go much deeper. For example, a psychology major might compare the behavior of the main character in *Bruce Almighty* with the classic traits of a person suffering from Attention Deficit Disorder. A theology student could compare the way God is portrayed in the film with God as revealed in the New Testament, while a literature student would be more likely to compare the plot of the movie with a plot found in Shakespeare or Dickens. An art major might compare the use of lighting in the movie with the way light and shadows are used in a famous painting.

Writing such a detailed and in-depth comparison will draw on all the skills learned in previous chapters while forcing writers to apply the knowledge and skills of their discipline to the world in which they live. Here are some guidelines for watching it.

HOW TO WATCH A MOVIE

1. Do not expect to be entertained. Stay alert to every detail of the movie and come prepared to take notes as you watch.

2. Read reviews and watch trailers so you know what to expect and can gain the most from the viewing.

3. If you have read the book, do not expect the movie to be like the book. They are different media. Movies cannot do everything books can, although some try. Both the *Harry Potter* and *Lord of the Rings* movies attempt to be faithful to the books. Modern special effects help make this possible.

4. Ignore the box office charts. Movies are not a sport, and the weekend's top film has won nothing except a lot of money. Not everyone willing to spend money on movies has your good taste.

5. Be aware that *everything* in a movie is deliberate. Shots are filmed until the director is satisfied that his vision has been accurately recorded. Every movement of the frame and within the frame has a purpose. Ask yourself why each shot looks the way it does. Why is there a close-up here, a two-shot there? Common sense often dictates these things. A scene at a party might start with a shot of all the guests, then cut to a closer look at two guests deep in conversation, then cut to a close-up of a third person who notices that they are talking. The director needs to keep you oriented to what is going on as well as

show you (tell you?) how to feel and think about every situation.

6. Be aware of symbols and their potential interpretations. A symbol is an image that creates a resonance in your mind. What does it symbolize? That depends on you and your mind. A dollar sign might symbolize wealth to you, greed to me, security to her, a mere price tag to him. The nice thing is that you can never be wrong about a symbol as long as you know what it means to you. You can only *speculate* on what it means to the director and actor, but you can *know* what it means to you.

7. Look for three kinds of action: internal, external, and symbolic. Internal action concerns the thoughts and feelings of characters. External action refers to all the actions taken by the characters. Symbolic action refers to *how* things are done to represent a deeper meaning. If the boy kills the mouse and then laughs, it means something very different than if he kills the mouse because he must, and then weeps.

8. Notice the soundtrack. Be aware of how music is used to create mood and trigger emotions. Think about whether the sounds improve or detract from your viewing experience.

9. Realize that all good movies inspire conversations, rehashes, and arguments. Much of what you learn from a movie will come from discussions afterward with others who saw it.

10. Use both sides of your brain. The right side of your brain is devoted to sensory impressions, colors, music, and emotion. The left side of your brain deals with abstract thought, logic, philosophy, and analysis. A great movie will engage your right brain while you are watching it. It will engage your left brain after you have watched it.

THE ELEMENTS OF LITERATURE

Writing comparison papers based on a movie gives students experience integrating artistic and media events into scholarly research. The process of using material from a movie is not that different from using similar material from traditional literature or other print publications. Teachers of literature generally expect students to write about what they read. Below are typical things they look for:

1. Show how an author handled one element of a story.

2. Compare how two different works treat a particular element.

3. Weigh several elements and then determine the writer's intention.

4. Air your reactions to some work.

Most writing assignments in literature feature one or more of the following elements: characterization, plot, point of view, setting, symbols, irony, and theme. Contemplate these concepts and answer the questions regarding these elements as you watch a movie. You are taking notes that will equip you to write an informed and effective paper.

Characterization: Authors deliberately develop their characters in a way that conveys a particular message or perspective. The better you understand the characters, the more accurately you will be able to analyze the literature as a whole. Most literature has a protagonist as well as a large assortment of other characters. Some of the questions to ask when studying characterization include the following:

1. How do the characters in a story behave?

2. What do they look like?

3. Where do their thoughts tend to linger?

4. What do they value in life?

5. How do they talk?

6. How do other people respond to them?

7. What are their personal habits?

Plot: Plot is the series of events that moves a narrative along. The stage is set, characters are introduced, and conflicts develop. Action gradually builds to a climax where events take a decisive turn and conflict is resolved in some way.

To organize plots, writers use several techniques. In foreshadowing, for example, the writer hints at later developments, thus creating interest and building suspense. When using flashback, the writer interrupts the flow of events to relate happenings that occurred before the point at which the story opened, then resumes the narrative at or near the point of interruption. Before writing about plot, answer these questions:

1. What are the key events of the story?
   Do they unfold in a conventional way or deviate from it in some way?

2. Identify where the writer uses foreshadowing or flashback.
   What purpose is achieved with these techniques?

3. Is the plot believable and effective, or weak in some way?

4. What are unique features of the plot?

5. Is this plot similar to another story with which you are familiar?

6. Select plot features to write about.

Point of View: This is the vantage point from which the writer views events. In first-person narration, someone in the work tells what happens. A third-person narrator stays completely out of the story. Most third-person narrators reveal the thoughts of just one character. Others, with limited omniscience, can enter the heads of several characters, while others display full omniscience and know everything. In contemporary fiction there is also another type of third-person narration—dramatic— in which a dramatic narrator moves about like a movie camera recording the actions and words of characters without revealing thoughts. Stories with surprise endings often use this technique. Explore these questions when writing about point of view:

1. What point of view is used? Why?
2. Is it suitable for the situation? Why or why not?
3. If the narration is first person, is the narrator reliable? What textual evidence supports the answer?
4. What focus would produce an effective paper? What textual evidence could support its discussion?

Setting: Setting locates characters in time, place, and culture so they can think, feel, and act against this background. Ask these questions about setting:

1. What are its key features?
2. What does the setting accomplish (create mood, reveal character, serve as a symbol, reinforce a point)? How does it accomplish these things?
3. In what ways does the setting seem realistic? If it does not seem realistic, why not?
4. What focus and textual evidence would produce an effective paper?

Symbols: Names, persons, objects, places, colors, or actions that have significance beyond their surface meaning are symbols. They can be very obvious (Mr. Grimm) or subtle, as an object representing a universal human emotion.

A <u>private</u> symbol has special significance within a literary work but not outside it. For example, in *The Shattered Urn*, an allegory where a ceramic urn represents marriage, it is highly symbolic of the condition of his marriage when "Lord William shattered that urn with a rock the size of his heart. But Delightla gathered up the pieces… (Runyon D. 95).

Conventional symbols are deeply rooted in culture, and almost everyone knows what they represent. The woman who wears a gold cross on a necklace symbolizes something very different from the man who has a swastika or devil's head tattoo on his shoulder. Answer these questions concerning symbols:

1. What symbols are used and where do they appear?
2. Are they *private* or *conventional*?
3. What do they appear to mean?
4. Do any of them undergo a change in meaning? If so, how and why?
5. Which symbol(s) could I discuss effectively?
6. What textual evidence would support my interpretation?

Irony: Ironic features are discrepancies between appearance and reality, expectation and outcome. Sometimes a character says one thing but means something else. When a college student tumbles out of bed, directly into yesterday's clothes, and out into the world without so much as a look in the mirror, a comment by a classmate that "you look great today" is probably thick with irony. Irony also results when the reader or a character recognizes something as important, but another character does not. Answer these questions regarding irony:

1. Where does irony occur?
2. What does it accomplish?
3. What could my thesis be, and how could I support it?

Theme: The theme is the controlling idea, observation, or insight about life conditions or terms of living (such as evil, pride, love). Many literary works suggest several themes—sometimes one primary motif and several related ones. Realize that the theme may not be stated at all. Rather, you figure it out based on the characters, action, setting and other components of the story. For example, a student might argue that the theme of Shakespeare's *Romeo and Juliet* is to emphasize the inherent dangers of dishonesty and disobedience. Ask these questions:

1. What are the themes of this work? Which of these should I write about? Are they stated or unstated?
2. If stated, what elements support them?
3. If unstated, what elements create them?
4. What, if any, thematic weaknesses are present?

Supplement your notes on the elements of literature with additional information gained by researching the authors, producers, and actors in the movie. Then it will be time to write the comparison paper. For guidelines on how to document a movie, look on page 273 under "films" in the index of the *MLA Handbook*.

RESEARCH USING BLOOM'S TAXONOMY

You will need additional sources of information to give credibility to your paper. The comparison essay is not intended merely for you to state your opinion, but to demonstrate that your opinion is valid. Therefore, to expand on an earlier example, the psychology student claiming that a character suffers from Attention Deficit Disorder will need to quote sources explaining the meaning and symptoms of this disorder. This is an opportunity for you to make further discoveries in your own field of growing expertise while also making application of that knowledge to the world around you.

The first level of writing literature reviews (covered in previous chapters) is to summarize, paraphrase, and quote from a source. This touches on the first two levels of learning as outlined in Bloom's Taxonomy. Bloom identified six levels of understanding from the simple recall or recognition of facts at the lowest level through increasingly more complex and abstract mental levels to the highest order classified as evaluation (Dalton).

Assignment: Select a source containing valuable information to include in your comparison paper. Study that source in depth, read footnotes or endnotes, and look up in a reliable dictionary any words you do not understand. Then write a literature review that includes the following:

1 & 2: Knowledge and Comprehension:
Knowledge is the ability to recall or recognize information as it is learned. **Comprehension** reflects the ability to understand the material without relating it to anything else. Show your knowledge and comprehension by briefly summarizing the source. If it is fiction, explain to your audience who the characters are and what they represent (choose a particular audience you wish to speak to).

_____

_____

_____

_____

3, 4 & 5: Application, Analysis, and Synthesis:
Application means using the information to solve a problem with a single correct answer. **Analysis** means breaking information down into its component parts. **Synthesis** is creating something new from parts not

previously related. Demonstrate your ability to apply, analyze, and synthesize the information in your source. It may help to ponder these questions: What problem does this information solve? What did the material *mean* to the author and to his immediate audience? What is it likely to mean to readers today? What does it mean to you? How is the information useful today?

_____

_____

_____

_____

6. Evaluation: The last level in Bloom's Taxonomy reflects the ability to make judgments, put opinions in order, and apply standards. Appraise the quality and success of the material, perhaps comparing it with other similar materials that are more (or less) effective in achieving the same goals. How is this material useful in strengthening your comparison paper?

_____

_____

_____

_____

PEER REVIEW: Have a fellow student read and evaluate the comparison paper. It will be ideal if that student has also written a comparison paper about the same movie.

Classification (from chapter 6)

1. Has the author classified the aspect of the movie in question (placed it in a category or genre)?

   ____yes ____no

   If not, suggest a category: _____

2. Has the author classified the thing the movie is being compared with?

   ____yes ____no

A. Are they in the same class or category? If so, this paper should compare similarities.

B. Are they in different classes or categories? If so, this paper should contrast differences.

Comparison: Showing Relationships

3. Is the comparison using the block pattern or the alternating pattern?

   ____ block ____ alternating ____ both

4. Does the author use an analogy or illustration (from chapter 5)? ____ yes ____no

If not, is one needed to help the reader understand this comparison?

5. Does the paper consider all points of similarity and difference that relate to its purpose?

6. Are the comparisons arranged effectively?

Writing About Literature

7. Identify the elements of literature being compared in this paper and write them in the margins of the paper at appropriate places. Circle all that apply.

character   plot   point of view   setting

symbols   irony   theme

8. Identify the types of action being compared in this paper and write them in the margins of the paper at appropriate places. Circle all that apply.

external action   internal action   symbolic action

9. Evaluate how successfully the writer has applied Bloom's Taxonomy to the additional sources used: evaluation, synthesis, analysis, application, understanding, knowledge.

10. Identify points where you feel additional application of Bloom's Taxonomy would strengthen the paper.

General Evaluation

11. Read just the introduction and the conclusion. Edit so the two paragraphs hang together.

12. Help with transitions so each paragraph clearly and smoothly relates to those that precede and follow it.

13. Fix sentences that are not clearly expressed or logically constructed.

14. Omit needless words.

15. What can be done to make this comparison smell, taste, feel, look, and sound better?

_____

_____

_____

16. A minimum of four sources are required. (The movie itself is one of them.) How appropriate are the three additional sources to the point of this paper? Suggest changes if needed.

_____

_____

_____

17. Review the MLA format, punctuation and grammar, and content of parenthetical references and Works Cited for accuracy.

PLANNING THE REWRITE

Rewrite this paper and turn it in to the professor when due. At about this point students frequently ask, "How do I cite indirect sources—information found in one source but originating in another source?" In most scholarly work writers are required to go back to the original source and cite only that reference. Once they pull the original source and have looked up the reference and read it for themselves, they have verified the accuracy and can avoid mentioning the path leading them to that source. However, some professors permit undergraduate students to cite the original source and then add, "qtd. in...." An example is provided in the footnote below.[13] See the *MLA Handbook* page 226 for additional guidance.

A second difficulty with this rewrite may have to do with questions on how to document quotes within movies or quotes by reviewers. See *MLA Handbook* B. 1.6 for how to format a review footnote, and see "films" in the index (page 273) for guidance in locating documentation guidelines for a movie.

---

[13] Hypothetical example of one source quoting a second source: C. S. Lewis, *The Four Loves* (Oxford: Clarendon, 1967) 59, qtd. in Howard Snyder and Daniel Runyon, *Decoding The Church: Mapping the DNA of Christ's Body* (Grand Rapids: Baker, 2002) 218.

AVOIDING PLAGIARISM EXERCISE

Write the following quote in your own words:

"There is enough light for those who want to see and enough darkness for those of a contrary disposition."

—Pascal

_____

_____

_____

_____

_____

_____

_____

CHAPTER 8: MEDIA ANALYSIS

The ability to analyze the media became a vital skill with the development of the "mass media" in the past few centuries. No such thing existed prior to the 1440s when Johann Gutenberg introduced movable type in Germany. The influence of Gutenberg's printing abilities was recognized immediately, and authorities quickly erected barriers to control its influence on public opinion. Printers and writers in the English-speaking world struggled until 1700 to win the mere right to print. They fought for another century to protect that liberty and to win the right to criticize in print. The right to report news came equally slowly.

The freedom to print, to criticize, and to report in a way that defends the people's right to know is continually challenged today. In the United States, freedom of the press is intertwined with other basic freedoms—freedom of speech, freedom of assembly, and freedom of petition. Upon these freedoms rests the freedom of religious expression, freedom of political thought and action, and freedom of intellectual growth and communication of information and ideas.

The founding fathers of the United States worked to create a society with a government of the people, by the people, and for the people. The media is the chief instrument though which any such society can talk to itself, and therefore the people will fail to govern themselves successfully when they lose the ability to intelligently evaluate the accuracy, fairness, and truthfulness of the media.

The media has evolved from the printing press through radio, television, and the internet, but the premise remains the same, as explained by Thomas Jefferson, third President of the United States, in a letter to Richard Price: "Whenever the people are well informed, they can be trusted with their own government." Jefferson's confidence in the value of the free marketplace of thought is revealed in this letter:

I am persuaded that the good sense of the people will always be found to be the best army. They may be led astray for a moment, but will soon correct themselves. The people are the only censors of their governors; and even their errors will tend to keep these to the true principles of their institution. To punish these errors too severely would be to suppress the only safeguard of the public liberty. The way to prevent these irregular interpositions of the people, is to give them full information of their affairs through the channel of the public papers, and to contrive that those papers should penetrate to the whole mass of the people. The basis of our government being the opinion of the people, the very first object should be to keep that right; and were it left to me to decide whether we should have a government without newspapers, or newspapers without a government, I should not hesitate a moment to prefer the latter.[14]

The internet has created a global communications network making it vital for people in any country with access to that information to learn the skills of media analysis. All the writing and thinking techniques taught in this text must be brought into play here. Writing the media analysis essay will draw on **narrative** writing, **description** skills, and the ability to **define** and **illustrate** a concept. The ability to **classify** information

---

[14] Jefferson wrote many variations on this theme over a 19-year span from 1792-1811. The occasions included letters to George Hammond, May 29, 1792; William Duane, Mar. 28, 1811; and to Congress, Dec. 2, 1806. This hand-written letter is available for viewing online at <http://memory.loc.gov/ammem/collections/jefferson_papers> .

and understand **process** also plays an important role in successful media analysis.

A media event is anything that happens and is reported in any media format. One such event occurred on Saturday, March 4, 1865, in Washington, D.C., when President Abraham Lincoln delivered his Second Inaugural Address. Weeks of wet weather had turned Pennsylvania Avenue into a sea of mud and standing water where thousands of citizens stood to hear him speak. It was a troubled time dominated by years of civil war. In little more than a month, the President would be assassinated.

Abraham Lincoln's Second Inaugural Address

Fellow-Countrymen:

At this second appearing to take the oath of the Presidential office there is less occasion for an extended address than there was at the first. Then a statement somewhat in detail of a course to be pursued seemed fitting and proper. Now, at the expiration of four years, during which public declarations have been constantly called forth on every point and phase of the great contest which still absorbs the attention and engrosses the energies of the nation, little that is new could be presented. The progress of our arms, upon which all else chiefly depends, is as well known to the public as to myself, and it is, I trust, reasonably satisfactory and encouraging to all. With high hope for the future, no prediction in regard to it is ventured.

On the occasion corresponding to this four years ago all thoughts were anxiously directed to an impending civil war. All dreaded it, all sought to avert it. While the inaugural address was being delivered from this place, devoted altogether to saving the Union without war, urgent agents were in the city seeking to destroy it without war—seeking to dissolve the Union and divide effects by negotiation. Both parties deprecated war, but one of them would make war rather than let the nation survive, and the other would accept war rather than let it perish, and the war came.

One-eighth of the whole population were colored slaves, not distributed generally over the Union, but localized in the southern part of it. These slaves constituted a peculiar and powerful interest. All knew that this interest was somehow the cause of the war. To strengthen, perpetuate, and extend this interest was the object for which the insurgents would rend the Union even by war, while the

Government claimed no right to do more than to restrict the territorial enlargement of it.

Neither party expected for the war the magnitude or the duration which it has already attained. Neither anticipated that the cause of the conflict might cease with or even before the conflict itself should cease. Each looked for an easier triumph, and a result less fundamental and astounding. Both read the same Bible and pray to the same God, and each invokes His aid against the other. It may seem strange that any men should dare to ask a just God's assistance in wringing their bread from the sweat of other men's faces, but let us judge not, that we be not judged.

The prayers of both could not be answered. That of neither has been answered fully. The Almighty has His own purposes. "Woe unto the world because of offenses; for it must needs be that offenses come, but woe to that man by whom the offense cometh." If we shall suppose that American slavery is one of those offenses which, in the providence of God, must needs come, but which, having continued through His appointed time, He now wills to remove, and that He gives to both North and South this terrible war as the woe due to those by whom the offense came, shall we

170

discern therein any departure from those divine attributes which the believers in a living God always ascribe to Him?

Fondly do we hope, fervently do we pray, that this mighty scourge of war may speedily pass away. Yet, if God wills that it continue until all the wealth piled by the bondsman's two hundred and fifty years of unrequited toil shall be sunk, and until every drop of blood drawn with the lash shall be paid by another drawn with the sword, as was said three thousand years ago, so still it must be said "the judgments of the Lord are true and righteous altogether."

With malice toward none, with charity for all, with firmness in the right as God gives us to see the right, let us strive on to finish the work we are in, to bind up the nation's wounds, to care for him who shall have borne the battle and for his widow and his orphan, to do all which may achieve and cherish a just and lasting peace among ourselves and with all nations.

ANALYSIS QUESTIONS

1. Write a paragraph exploring how TV commentators would likely respond today if they were covering this very short inaugural address.

2. Write your reaction to the fact that President Lincoln quotes the Bible, talks about the sovereignty of God, and explores the complexities of unanswered prayer as integral parts of this auspicious speech.

3. The theme of "just war" underlies Lincoln's thoughts. How should this concept play into any interpretation of this media event?

MEDIA ANALYSIS READINGS

If "media" can be broadly defined as "news" of any public event, then it occurred daily in the ancient world, and public opinion flourished although it had no technology to quickly spread such opinions around the globe. The arrest and murder of Jesus is perhaps the most notorious media event ever recorded by eyewitnesses. Excerpts of Matthew's account appear below along with analysis questions to help modern readers apply media analysis skills to the event.

Matthew 26:1-16

And so this is what happened, *finally*. Jesus finished all His teaching, and He said to His disciples,

Jesus: [2] The feast of Passover begins in two days. That is when the Son of Man is handed over to be crucified.

³ *And almost as He spoke,* the chief priests were getting together with the elders at the home of the high priest, Caiaphas. ⁴ They schemed *and mused* about how they could *trick Jesus,* sneak around and capture Him, and then kill Him.

Chief Priests: ⁵ We shouldn't try to catch Him at the great public festival. The people would riot *if they knew what we were doing.*

⁶ Meanwhile Jesus was at Bethany staying at the home of Simon the leper. ⁷ *While He was at Simon's house,* a woman came to see Him. She had an alabaster flask of very valuable ointment with her, and as Jesus reclined at the table, she poured the ointment on His head. ⁸ The disciples, seeing this scene, were furious.

Disciples: This is an absolute waste! ⁹ The woman could have sold that ointment for lots of money, and then she could have given it to the poor.

¹⁰ Jesus knew what the disciples were saying among themselves, *so He took them to task.*

Jesus: Why don't you leave this woman alone? She has done a good thing. ¹¹ *It is good that you are concerned about the poor,* but the poor will always be with you—I will not be. ¹² In pouring this ointment on My body, she has prepared Me for My burial. ¹³ I tell you this: the good news *of the kingdom of God* will be spread all over the world, *and wherever the good news travels,* people will tell the story of this woman and her good discipleship. And people will remember her.

[14] At that, one of the twelve, Judas Iscariot, went to the chief priests.

Judas Iscariot: [15] What will you give me to turn Him over to you?

They offered him 30 pieces of silver. [16] And from that moment, he began to watch for a chance to betray Jesus.

ANALYSIS QUESTIONS

4. Identify which characters described above genuinely understood what was going on, and summarize what each one apparently understood about the event.

5. Identify which characters have the greatest influence on how the event is portrayed by the "media." Summarize what you think their "spin" will be.

Matthew 26:57-68

[57] The crowd that had arrested Jesus took Him to Caiaphas, the high priest. The scribes and elders had gathered *at Caiaphas's house and were waiting for*

Jesus to be delivered. [58] Peter followed Jesus (though at some distance *so as not to be seen*). He slipped into Caiaphas's house and attached himself to a group of servants. And he sat watching, waiting to see how things would unfold.

[59] The high priest and his council of advisors first produced *false evidence against Jesus*—false evidence meant to justify some charge and Jesus' execution. [60] But even though many men were willing to lie, the council couldn't come up with the evidence it wanted. Finally, two men stood up.

Two Men: [61] Look, He said, "I can destroy God's temple and rebuild it in three days." *What more evidence do you need?*

[62] Then Caiaphas the high priest stood up and addressed Jesus.

Caiaphas: Aren't You going to respond to these charges? What exactly are these two men accusing You of?

[63] Jesus remained silent.

Caiaphas *(to Jesus)***:** Under a sacred oath before the living God, tell us plainly: are You the Anointed One, the Son of God?

Jesus: [64] So you *seem to be* saying. I will say this: beginning now, you will see the Son of Man sitting at the right hand of God's power and glory and coming on heavenly clouds.

⁶⁵ The high priest tore his robes *and screeched*.

Caiaphas: Blasphemy! We don't need any more witnesses—we've all just witnessed this most grievous blasphemy, *right here and now*. ⁶⁶ So, gentlemen, what's your verdict?

Gentlemen: He deserves to die.

⁶⁷ Then they spat in His face and hit Him. Some of them smacked Him, slapped Him across the cheeks, ⁶⁸ and jeered.

Some of the Men: Well, Anointed One, prophesy for us, *if You can*—who hit You? *And who is about to hit You next?*

ANALYSIS QUESTION

6. This report comes from Matthew, a disciple of Jesus. How might an official report from the Chief Priest read differently? What details might be added or eliminated, and why would they be likely to make these changes?

Matthew 27:11-26

¹¹ Jesus was standing before the governor, *Pilate*.

Pilate: Are You the King of the Jews?

Jesus: So you say.

[12] The chief priests and the elders *stood and poured out their accusations: that Jesus was a traitor, a seditious rebel, a crazy, a would-be Savior, and a would-be king.* Jesus stood in the stream of accusations, but He did not respond.

Pilate: [13] Do You hear these accusations they are making against You?

[14] Still Jesus said nothing, which Pilate found rather astounding—*no protests, no defense, nothing.*

[15] Now the governor had a custom. During the *great Jewish* festival *of* Passover, he would allow the crowd to pick one of the condemned men, and he, *Pilate,* would set the man free. *Just like that. Gratuitous, gracious freedom.* [16] At this time, they had a notorious prisoner named Barabbas. [17] So when the crowd gathered, Pilate offered them a choice:

Pilate: Whom do you want me to free? Barabbas or Jesus, whom some call the Anointed One?

[18] Pilate knew the chief priests and elders hated Jesus and had delivered Him up because they envied Him.

[19] Then Pilate sat down on his judgment seat, and he received a message from his wife: "Distance yourself utterly from *the proceedings against* this righteous man. I have had a dream about Him, a dream full of

twisted sufferings—*He is innocent, I know it, and we should have nothing to do with Him.*"

[20] But the chief priests and the elders convinced the crowd to demand that Barabbas, not Jesus, *whom-some-call-the-Anointed-One*, be freed and that Jesus be put to death.

Pilate *(standing before the crowd)*: [21] Which of these men would you have me free?

Crowd *(shouting)*: Barabbas!

Pilate: [22] What would you have me do with this Jesus, whom some call the Anointed One?

Crowd *(shouting)*: Crucify Him!

Pilate: [23] Why? What crime has this man committed?

Crowd *(responding with a shout)*: Crucify Him!

[24] Pilate saw that unless he wanted a riot on his hands, he now had to bow to their wishes. So he took *a pitcher of* water, stood before the crowd, and washed his hands.

Pilate: You will see to this crucifixion, for this man's blood will be *upon you* and not upon me. *I wash myself of it.*

Crowd: [25] Indeed, let His blood be upon us—upon us and our children!

[26] So Pilate released Barabbas, and he had Jesus flogged and handed over to be crucified.

ANALYSIS QUESTION

7. How is the system of justice presided over by Pilate similar to the way prisoners are treated where you live? How is it different?

Matthew 27:35-44

[35] And so they had Him crucified. They divided the clothes off His back by drawing lots,[b] [36] and they sat on the ground and watched Him *hang*. [37] They placed a sign over His head: "This is Jesus, King of the Jews." [38] And then they crucified two thieves next to Him, one at His right hand and one at His left hand.

[39] Passersby shouted curses and blasphemies at Jesus. They wagged their heads *at Him and hissed.*

Passersby: [40] You're going to destroy the temple and then rebuild it in three days? Why don't You start with saving Yourself? Come down from the cross if You can, if You're God's Son.

Chief Priests, Scribes, and Elders *(mocking Him)*: [41-42] He saved others, but He can't save Himself. If He's really the King of Israel, then let Him climb down from the cross—then we'll believe Him. [43] He claimed communion with God—well, let God save Him, if He's God's beloved Son.

[44] Even the thieves hanging to His right and left poured insults upon Him. [45] And then, starting at noon, the entire land became dark. It was dark for three hours. [46] In the middle of the dark afternoon, Jesus cried out in a loud voice.

ANALYSIS QUESTIONS

8. Some countries do not permit more than one point of view when reporting such an event. What sort of trouble might Matthew be in if he publishes this portrayal of the behavior of the religious authorities?

9. If not published for the general public, how might this information be circulated?

Matthew 27:62-66

[62] The next day, which is the day after the Preparation Day, the chief priests and the Pharisees went together to Pilate. [63] They reminded him that when Jesus was alive He had claimed that He would be raised from the dead after three days.

Chief Priests and Pharisees: [64] So please order someone to secure the tomb for at least three days. Otherwise His disciples might sneak in and steal His body away, and then claim that He has been raised from the dead. If that happens, then we would have been better off just leaving Him alive.

Pilate: [65] You have a guard. Go and secure the grave. [66] So they went to the tomb, sealed the stone in its mouth, and left the guard to keep watch.

ANALYSIS QUESTION

10. This passage models the common practice of authorities who tend to want to put a "spin" or bias on public opinion to justify their own actions. Evaluate the actions of both the Pharisees and Pilate in this regard.

   A. Actions taken by the Pharisees:

   B. Actions taken by Pilate:

Matthew 28:1-10

   After the Sabbath, as the light of the next day, the first day of the week, crept over Palestine, Mary Magdalene and the other Mary came to the tomb *to keep vigil.* [2] Earlier there had been an earthquake. A messenger of the Lord had come down from heaven and had gone to the grave. He rolled away the stone and sat down on top of it. [3] He *veritably* glowed. He was vibrating with light. *His clothes were light,* white *like transfiguration,* like fresh snow. [4] The soldiers guarding the tomb were terrified. They froze like stone. [5] The messenger spoke to the women, *to Mary Magdalene and the other Mary.*

Messenger of the Lord: Don't be afraid. I know you are here keeping watch for Jesus who was crucified. [6] But Jesus is not here. He was raised, just as He said He would be. Come over to the grave, and see for yourself. [7] And then go straight to His disciples, and tell them He's been raised from the dead and has gone on to Galilee. You'll find Him there. Listen carefully to what I am telling you.

[8] The women were both terrified and thrilled, and they quickly left the tomb and went to find the disciples and give them this *outstandingly good* news. [9] But while they were on their way, they saw Jesus Himself.

Jesus *(greeting the women)***:** Rejoice.

The women fell down before Him, kissing His feet and worshiping Him.

Jesus: [10] Don't be afraid. Go and tell My brothers to go to Galilee. Tell them I will meet them there.

ANALYSIS QUESTION

11. Matthew may not have been at all the events described above, but as one of the disciples "they ran

to tell," he would have been among the first to hear the report. Compare his situation with that of a modern reporter who must interview eyewitnesses to get a report.

Matthew 28:11-15

[11] As the women were making their way to the disciples, some of the soldiers who had been standing guard *by Jesus' tomb recovered themselves*, went to the city, and told the chief priests everything that had happened—*the earthquake just after dawn, the heavenly messenger, and his commission to the Marys.* [12] The chief priests gathered together all the elders, *an emergency conference of sorts. They needed a plan. They decided the simplest course was bribery:* they would pay off the guards [13] and order them to say that the disciples had come in the middle of the night and had stolen Jesus' corpse while they slept. [14] The chief priests promised the soldiers they would run interference with the governor so that the soldiers wouldn't be punished *for falling asleep when they were supposed to be keeping watch.* [15] The guards took the bribe and spread the story around town—and indeed, you can still find people today who will tell you *that Jesus did not really rise from*

the dead, that it was a trick, some sort of sleight of hand.

ANALYSIS QUESTIONS

12. Is understanding and interpreting an event that occurred more than a century ago easier than evaluating a current event in the same way? Answer "yes" or "no" and explain why.

13. Imagine the difficulties modern media analysts would encounter if they faced trying to understand the crucifixion. What would they be most likely to misunderstand about this event? Why?

14. Tell a true story from your own experience where you know the truth was different from that which was generally accepted as true.

15. How did Matthew's skill as a discerning media analyst help assure the accuracy of the Bible?

16. How will you imitate the work of Matthew in order to write your own perceptive and reliable media analysis paper?

WRITING ASSIGNMENT

It doesn't matter whether the media critics are standing in the mud listening to Abraham Lincoln's Second Inaugural Address in person, witnessing the resurrection of Jesus from the dead, or reading an editorial on an internet blog. Whether the media event is a speech, a TV show, a news clip, or an article in a newspaper or magazine, the questions wise media analysts ask and the notes they take are similar and should include those suggested in the form below.

In order to fill out this form, it is first necessary to identify the media event you wish to evaluate. Select a recent happening in your field of interest. You will most likely find this information in a scholarly journal devoted to your field of study or a specialized internet news service focused on your discipline. Do not use a movie for your media event since that was the subject of the assignment for the last chapter. However, any other media event is a fair target, whether in print or visual media. Once you have located a media event of great personal interest, write the information requested below in a journal or computer file.

Name of production or name of article

_____

Authors _____

Names of important people

_____

Names of important places

_____

Dates and locations of important events

_____

Key ideas and themes presented

_____

Summary of production

_____

_____

_____

_____

Media analysis questions to consider:

1. How is the production structured?

2. What is the author/producer trying to say? Paraphrase a key element of the content.

3. What is the author's bias or worldview? That is to say, what are you being told to believe, or what "spin" is placed on the facts presented?

4. What are your personal feelings and reaction to the work?

5. Now that you have collected useful notes, you are ready for the prewriting exercise.

PRE-WRITING EXERCISE

1. Accurately document the media event/article you will critique based on guidelines in the *MLA Handbook* by writing a Works Cited entry in correct format.

2. Do you understand the *assumptions* (worldview) that shape the production being analyzed? Are the assumptions stated or unstated? What are they?

3. What is the fundamental argument of the media event being analyzed?

4. Is the argument *valid*: does the conclusion *necessarily* follow? (See Chapter 10 for a discussion of what constitutes a valid argument.) Outline the argument.

5. If the argument is valid, are the premises to the argument *true*? Identify the premises.

6. Can you identify any *logical fallacies* in the media production being analyzed? (See Chapter 10 for a list of logical fallacies and their definitions.) List them.

7. How will you take advantage of the logical fallacies to make your own argument stronger? Be sure you do not fall into logical fallacies of your own.

Give Your Analysis Credibility

Now you are ready to write your analysis of the media event. By the time you finish the first draft of your essay, it should become clear that you are not a recognized authority on the topic you have chosen to address. Therefore, you do not have the credibility to make the claims you may wish to make.

The way to gain credibility is to align yourself with authorities in your field of study who are respected experts. Skilled writers know how to back up a point they want to make by identifying it with what the experts have already said. This is the beauty and value of research. To say "I think that …" has practically no value compared with being able to write, "Einstein's theory of relativity provides convincing evidence that…."

To carry out your research, follow the "Research Using Bloom's Taxonomy" guidelines provided in Chapter 7. Assume that you will be required to turn in three literature reviews along with the final paper (show your work!). Be sure to use accurate parenthetical references with every source you use, and include each source in the Works Cited, just as you learned to do on all previous writing assignments. Make sure to carefully follow all formatting and punctuation guidelines provided in the *MLA Handbook.*

PEER REVIEW: Have a fellow student read and evaluate the media analysis following these guidelines:

1. Read the entire essay.

a. As you read, bracket each section of **objective** information and write "objective" or "facts" in the margin. (Review Chapter One for a summary of objective, subjective, and interpretive information.)

b. Bracket each section of **subjective** information and write "subjective" or "opinion" in the margin.

c. Bracket each section of **interpretive** information and write "interpretation" or "author's conclusion" in the margin.

_____ Check to make sure each piece of **objective** information is adequately documented (with correctly written parenthetical reference and bibliography).

_____ Check to make sure each piece of **subjective** information is sufficiently plausible, convincing, and adequately backed up with objective information.

_____ Check to make sure each piece of **interpretive** information has been arrived at *in a logical manner* and is adequately backed up with subjective and objective information.

2. Does the writer show evidence of truly understanding the *assumptions* (worldview) that shaped the production being analyzed? Are the assumptions

stated or unstated? What are they?

_____

_____

_____

3. If the writer is building some argument concerning the
   media event being analyzed, is the argument
   inductive or deductive?

Inductive argument follows some form of the
   scientific method that explores the extent to which a
   thing is *probably* true based on the evidence (see
   Chapter 11 for more details).

_____

_____

_____

Deductive argument follows a syllogism: If one thing is
   true, and if a second thing is true, then this
   conclusion is sound (see Chapter 10 for more details).
   If the argument is deductive, is the argument *valid*
   (does the conclusion n*ecessarily* follow)? Are the
   premises to the argument *true*?

_____

_____

_____

4. Can you identify any *logical fallacies* in the writer's analysis of the media production? (See Chapter 10 for a list of logical fallacies). If so, list them here:

_____

_____

_____

_____

5. Make suggestions to the author on how to improve this essay.

_____

_____

_____

PLANNING THE REWRITE

Your media analysis essay is based on published sources, and the ultimate goal of writing such a paper is to see it published. Therefore, it will be helpful at this time to compare your own writing with that of the published materials on which you based your work.

1. How does your writing style compare with the published articles? Is it better or worse? In what ways?

2. How does the content of your paper compare with the published articles?

3. How does your argument compare with the published articles? Is it more convincing, or less so? How can you tell?

INVISIBLE MAN

As you write your final draft, remember to employ the various writing skills encouraged in earlier chapters to make your paper powerful. When Ralph Ellison wrote *Invisible Man,* he used such skills to describe one aspect of a media event, a solo at a vespers service at a southern college. Notice his powers of description and his ability to capture the climate:

As the organ voices died, I saw a thin brown girl arise noiselessly with the rigid control of a modern dancer, high in the upper rows of the choir, and begin to sing a cappella. She began softly, as though singing to herself of emotions of utmost privacy, a sound not addressed to the gathering, but which they overheard almost against her will....

I saw the guests on the platform turn to look behind them, to see the thin brown girl in white choir robe standing high against the organ pipes, herself become before our eyes a pipe of contained, controlled and sublimated anguish, a thin plain face transformed by music. I could not understand the words, but only the mood, sorrowful, vague and ethereal, of the singing. It throbbed with nostalgia, regret and repentance, and I sat with a lump in my throat as she sank down; not a sitting but a controlled collapsing, as though she were balancing, sustaining the simmering bubble of her final tone by some delicate rhythm of her heart's blood, or by some mystic concentration of her being, focused upon the sound through the contained liquid of her large uplifted eyes. There was no applause, only the appreciation of a profound silence. (116-117)

With such writing Ellison has simultaneously analyzed the event and also pushed himself to a higher level of expression, capturing mood and feeling and spirit as well as facts. Use the insights above and the suggestions provided by the peer review for guidance as you rewrite your media analysis paper and turn it in for a grade.

SECTION III:
COLLEGE WRITING ARGUMENTS

Section 1 of *Integrated Reading and Writing* offered brief readings that modeled various writing techniques to give writers tools useful in crafting essays. Section II provided opportunities to read and experience media events and explore them by writing comparison and media analysis essays. Section III builds on the assertion of C. S. Lewis that "all possible knowledge depends on the validity of reasoning" (*Miracles* 26). This section teaches cause and effect, deductive, and inductive reasoning skills for building strong arguments.

The term "argument" is used only in the academic sense to mean "persuasion." Benjamin Franklin clarifies the difference in describing a relationship with friends:

We sometimes disputed, and very fond we were of argument, and very desirous of confuting one another, which is apt to become a very bad habit, making people extremely disagreeable in company. Thence, besides souring and spoiling conversation, argument produces disgust and enmity where you may have occasion for friendship. I had caught it by reading my father's books of dispute about religion. Persons of good sense, I have since observed, seldom fall into it." (*The Abridged Autobiography of Benjamin Franklin* 22)

Follow Franklin's advice by learning the art and craft of persuasive writing that wins over readers by force of reason and sound argument.

CHAPTER 9
CAUSE AND EFFECT ARGUMENT

Understanding cause and effect is basic to logic, and knowing how to think logically is the foundation for argument. This chapter explores the cause and effect system of reasoning. Chapter 10 moves beyond cause and effect to the "deductive argument" system of reasoning based on linear logic rooted in ancient Greek thought. Chapter 11 will explore the "inductive argument" thought process common in much of the world where Duane Elmer's observation rings true, that "people from various cultures reason differently" (150).

Cause and effect reasoning can result in persuasive writing. When it is established that one thing always results in another thing, it becomes possible to explain why things are as they are. Much scientific research is based on cause and effect reasoning, and it is possible that students who wrote a process paper based on the scientific method summarized in Chapter 3 were working primarily with a cause and effect situation.

Writing a cause and effect argument becomes somewhat complicated because things are seldom as simple as they appear. Consider this statement: "If a person heats water, then it will boil when it reaches 212 degrees Fahrenheit." This is a simple cause and effect statement. But it is only true at sea level, and water actually boils at increasingly lower temperatures at higher altitudes. People living at 5500 feet altitude in Colorado will find water boils there at about 202 degrees. This does not mean the cause and effect statement is wrong, just that it is conditional. Much of the work of writing in cause and effect format has to do with explaining all the conditions that make the original statement true.

Keep in mind that multiple causes often contribute to a single effect. Why is Ming-Yau six feet tall although his parents are only five feet tall? The cause is not only because he inherited the physique of his grandfather who was much taller than his mother, but also because he was given daily vitamins and nutritional food of excellent quality and variety throughout his formative years, whereas both of his parents had only a daily portion of rice to eat their first 15 years of life. To identify only one cause for the effect oversimplifies the situation.

Another frequent mistake is to assume that because one event occurs before another, the second effect was caused by the first action. A new leader is elected and then a drought causes economic hardship, but the election results most likely did not cause the drought, which would have come no matter which candidate was chosen.[15] Superstitions are often the result of this fallacy of apparent but not actual cause and effect.

Reasoning errors often occur when causes are confused with their effects. A young child might observe a tree limb swaying and believe it is making the wind blow. Adults with more knowledge of the world explain that actually it is the wind that causes the tree to sway. Yet on an even larger scale, the child may be right. Huge rain forests in Brazil create weather patterns by putting large volumes of moisture in the air which may in fact cause the wind to blow.

Finally, note the distinction between cause and effect from "ground and consequent." This distinction becomes obvious from two uses of the word "because." Consider the difference between "The professor is ill today because he ate shell fish yesterday" (cause/effect), and "The professor is ill today because he is still in bed" (ground/consequent) which only infers that he may be ill. Another example: "She screamed because it hurt"

---

[15] This is an example of the "Post hoc, ergo propter hoc" fallacy described in Chapter 10.

(cause/effect), and "It must have hurt because she screamed" (ground/consequent). Cause/effect indicates a dynamic connection whereas ground/consequent is a logical relation between the beliefs or statements.

Cause and effect drives the plot of many stories. Hermann, the protagonist in the famous Russian author Alexander Pushkin's short story *The Queen of Spades,* says in two places regarding his reluctance to gamble, "I am not in the position to sacrifice the necessary in the hope of winning the superfluous" (1, 10). When he violates this principle with an audacious gambling risk, his life is shattered. Pushkin comprehended the power of cause and effect reasoning and used it as the core of a powerful plot. It is equally useful as the core of a powerful college writing essay.

CAUSE AND EFFECT READINGS

1. **Analysis question:** Based on the readings below, make a chart that lists causes in the left hand column and their effects in the right hand column. Be careful to avoid the fallacies discussed above of multiple causes, confusing chronology with cause and effect, and mistaking effects for causes.

James 4:7-10

Submit yourselves to the one true God and fight against the devil *and his schemes.* If you do, he will run away *in failure.* [8] Come close to the one true God, and He will draw close to you. Wash your hands; you have dirtied them in sin. Cleanse your heart, because your mind is split down the middle, *your love for God on one side and selfish pursuits on the other.*

[9] Now is the time to lament, to grieve, and to cry. Dissolve your laughter into sobbing, and exchange your joy for depression. [10] Lay yourself *bare, facedown to the ground,* in humility before the Lord; and He will lift your head *so you can stand tall.*

James 4:7-10 Chart

Causes	Effects
_____	_____
_____	_____
_____	_____
_____	_____

John 3:1-21

Nicodemus was one of the Pharisees, a man with some clout among his people. [2] He came to Jesus under the cloak of darkness to question Him.

Nicodemus: Teacher, some of us have been talking. You are obviously a teacher who has come from God. The signs You are doing are proof that God is with You.

Jesus: [3] I tell you the truth: only someone who experiences birth for a second time can *hope to* see the kingdom of God.

Nicodemus: [4] *I am a grown man.* How can someone be born again when he is old *like me*? Am I to crawl back into my mother's womb for a second birth? *That's impossible!*

Jesus: [5] I tell you the truth, if someone does not experience water and Spirit birth, there's no chance he will make it into God's kingdom. [6] *Like from like.* Whatever is born from flesh is flesh; whatever is born from Spirit is spirit. [7] Don't be shocked by My words, *but I tell you the truth.* Even you, *an educated and respected man among your people,* must be reborn *by the Spirit to enter the kingdom of God.*

[8] The wind blows all around us as if it has a will of its own; we *feel and* hear it, but we do not understand where it has come from or where it will end up. Life in the Spirit is as if it were the wind of God.

Nicodemus: [9] I still do not understand how this can be.

Jesus: [10] Your responsibility is to instruct Israel *in matters of faith*, but you do not comprehend *the necessity of life in the Spirit*?

[11] I tell you the truth: we speak about the things we know, and we give evidence about the things we have seen, and you choose to reject *the truth of* our witness. [12] If you do not believe when I talk to you about ordinary, earthly realities, then heavenly realities will certainly elude you. [13] No one has ever journeyed to heaven above except the One who has come down from heaven—the Son of Man, who is of heaven.

[14] Moses lifted up the serpent in the wilderness. In the same way, the Son of Man must be lifted up; [15] then all those who believe in Him will experience everlasting life.

[16] For God expressed His love for the world in this way: He gave His only Son so that whoever believes in Him will not face everlasting destruction, but will have everlasting life. [17] Here's the point. God didn't send His Son into the world to judge it; instead, He is here to rescue a world *headed toward certain destruction*.

[18] No one who believes in Him has to fear condemnation, yet condemnation is already the reality for everyone who refuses to believe because they reject the name of the only Son of God.

[19] Why does God allow for judgment *and condemnation*? Because the Light, *sent from God,* pierced through the world's darkness *to expose ill motives, hatred, gossip, greed, violence, and the like.* Still some people preferred the darkness over the light because their actions were dark. [20] Some of humankind hated the light. They *scampered hurriedly* back into the darkness where vices thrive and wickedness flourishes. [21] Those who *abandon deceit and* embrace what is true, they will enter into the light where it will be clear that all their deeds come from God.

John 3 Chart

Causes	Effects
_____	_____
_____	_____
_____	_____
_____	_____

Genesis 3

Of all the wild creatures the Eternal God had created, the serpent was the craftiest.

Serpent *(to the woman)*: Is it true that God has forbidden you to eat *fruits* from the trees of the garden?

Eve: [2] *No, serpent. God said* we are free to eat the fruit from the trees in the garden. [3] *We are granted access to* *any variety and all amounts of fruit* with one exception: the fruit from the tree found in the center of the garden. God instructed us not to eat or touch the fruit of that tree or we would die.

Serpent: [4] *Die? No,* you'll not die. *God is playing games with you.* [5] *The truth is that* God knows the day you eat the fruit from that tree you will awaken *something powerful in you* and become like Him: possessing knowledge of *both* good and evil.

[6] The woman *approached the tree,* eyed its fruit, and coveted its *mouth-watering, wisdom-granting* beauty. She plucked a fruit from the tree and ate. She then offered *the fruit* to her husband who was close by, and he ate as well. [7] Suddenly their eyes were opened *to a reality previously unknown.* For the first time, they sensed *their vulnerability and rushed to hide* their naked bodies, stitching fig leaves into crude loincloths. [8] Then they heard the sound of the Eternal God walking in the cool *misting* shadows of the garden. The man and his wife took cover among the trees and hid from the Eternal God.

God *(calling to Adam)***:** [9] Where are you?

Adam: [10] When I heard the sound of You coming in the garden, I was afraid because I am naked. So I hid *from You.*

God: [11] Who told you that you are naked? Have you eaten from the tree *in the center of the garden,* the very one I commanded you not to eat from?

Adam *(pointing at the woman)***:** [12] *It was she!* The woman You gave me as a companion put the fruit in my hands, and I ate it.

God *(to the woman)***:** [13] What have you done?

Eve: It was the serpent! He tricked me, and I ate.

[14] **God** *(to the serpent)***:** What you have done carries great consequences. Now you are cursed more than cattle or wild beasts. You will writhe on your belly forever, consuming the dust *out of which man was made.* [15]I will make you and your brood enemies of the woman and all her children; The woman's child will stomp your head, and you will strike his heel.

[16] **God** (to the woman) *As a consequence of your actions,* I will increase your suffering—the pain of childbirth and the sorrow of bringing forth the next generation. You will desire your husband; *but rather than a companion,* he will be the dominant partner.

[17] **God** (to the man) Because you followed your wife's advice instead of My command and ate of the tree from which I had forbidden you to eat, cursed is the ground. For the rest of your life, you will fight for every crumb of food from the *crusty clump of* clay *I made you from.*

[18]*As you labor,* the ground will produce thorns and thistles, and you will eat the plants of the field. [19]Your brow will sweat for your mouth to taste *even a morsel of* bread until the day you return to the very ground I made you from. From dust you have come, and to dust you shall return.

[20] The man named his wife Eve because she was *destined to become* the mother of all living. [21] The Eternal God pieced together the skins *of animals* and made clothes for Adam and Eve to wear.

God: [22] Look, the human has become like one of Us, possessing the knowledge of good and evil. *If We don't do something,* he will reach out his hand and take *some of the fruit* from the tree of life, eat it, and live forever.

[23] So the Eternal God banished Adam *and Eve* from the garden of Eden *and exiled humanity from paradise, sentencing humans to laborious lives* working the very ground man came from. [24] After driving them out, He stationed winged guardians at the east end of the garden of Eden and set up a sword of flames which *alertly* turned back and forth to guard the way to the tree of life.

Genesis 3 Chart

Causes	**Effects**
_____	_____
_____	_____

Romans 5

Since we have been *acquitted and* made right through faith, we are able to experience *true and lasting* peace with God through our Lord Jesus, the Anointed One, *the Liberating King.* [2] Jesus leads us into a place of *radical* grace where we are able to celebrate the hope of experiencing God's glory. [3] And that's not all. We also celebrate in seasons of suffering because we know that when we suffer we develop endurance, [4] which shapes our characters. When our characters are refined, we learn what it means to hope *and anticipate God's goodness.* [5] And hope will never fail to satisfy our deepest need because the Holy Spirit that was given to us has flooded our hearts with God's love.

[6] When the time was right, the Anointed One died for all of us who were far from God, powerless, and weak. [7] Now it is rare to find someone willing to die for an upright person, although it's possible that someone may give up his life for one who is truly good. [8] But *think about this:* while we were wasting our lives in sin, God revealed His powerful love to us *in a tangible display*—the Anointed One died for us. [9] As a result, the

blood of Jesus has made us right with God now, and certainly we will be rescued by Him from God's wrath *in the future.* [10] If we were in the heat of combat with God when His Son reconciled us by laying down His life, then how much more will we be saved by Jesus' *resurrection* life? [11] In fact, we stand now reconciled *and at peace* with God. That's why we celebrate in God through our Lord Jesus, the Anointed.

[12] Consider this: sin entered our world through one man, *Adam;* and through sin, death followed *in hot pursuit*. Death spread rapidly to infect all people on the earth as they engaged in sin.

[13] Before God gave the law, sin existed, *but there was no way to account for it*. Outside the law, how could anyone be charged and found guilty of sin? [14] Still, death plagued all humanity from Adam to Moses, even those whose sin was of a different sort than Adam's. *You see, in God's plan,* Adam was a prototype of the One who comes *to usher in a new day*. [15] But the free gift of grace bears no resemblance to Adam's crime *that brings a death sentence to all of humanity; in fact, it is quite the opposite*. For if the one man's sin brings death to so many, how much more does the gift of God's *radical* grace extend to humanity since Jesus the Anointed offered His generous gift. [16] His free gift is nothing like

the scourge of the first man's sin. The judgment that fell because of one false step brought condemnation, but the free gift following countless offenses results in a favorable verdict—not guilty. [17] If one man's sin brought a reign of death—*that's Adam's legacy*—how much more will those who receive grace in abundance and the free gift of redeeming justice reign in life by means of one other man—Jesus the Anointed.

[18] So here is the result: as one man's sin brought about condemnation *and punishment* for all people, so one man's act of faithfulness makes all of us right with God and brings us to new life. [19] Just as through one man's *defiant* disobedience every one of us were made sinners, so through the *willing* obedience of the one man many of us will be made right.

[20] When the law came into the picture, sin grew and grew; but wherever sin grew and spread, God's grace was there in fuller, greater measure. *No matter how much sin crept in, there was always more grace.* [21] In the same way that sin reigned in the sphere of death, now grace reigns through God's restorative justice, *eclipsing death and* leading to eternal life through the Anointed One, Jesus our Lord, *the Liberating King.*

Romans 5 Chart

Causes	Effects
_____	_____
_____	_____
_____	_____
_____	_____

WRITING ASSIGNMENT

Select a topic on which to write a cause and effect argument. It should be related in some clear way to the papers written for previous assignments. The structure of this paper is what will make it unique. A successful cause and effect argument is one that meets this simple rule of logic: If A is true, then B is true. "If the soccer players don't drink enough water, they will get dehydrated." A biblical model comes from John 5:46 where Jesus says, "If you believed Moses, you would believe me, for he wrote about me." Another example is John 7:17 where Jesus says to some Jews at a feast, "If anyone chooses to do God's will, he will find out whether my teaching comes from God or whether I speak on my own."

1. Write a thesis statement in the form of cause and effect: If _____ is true, then _____ will be true. Writing this

thesis statement may take some brainstorming. Consider the various causes and their effects as they apply to your area of interest. Identify one cause that particularly concerns you, and list the potential effects.

Cause   **Effects**

_____   _____

                                       _____

                                       _____

                                       _____

                                       _____

Alternately, identify one effect that particularly interests you, and list the potential causes.

Causes   **Effect**

_____   _____

_____

_____

_____

_____

2. Now sketch out in your journal or on computer some practice sentences and paragraphs indicating the way your paper is likely to develop.

3. With the brainstorming complete, it is time to do research to find out the validity of the cause and

effect sequence you are exploring. To carry out your research, follow the "Research Using Bloom's Taxonomy" guidelines provided in Chapter 7. Assume that your professor will require three literature reviews along with the final paper (show your work!). Be sure to accurately document sources according to guidelines in the *MLA Handbook*.

4. Normally it takes two or three pages to successfully explore and explain a cause and effect sequence to the satisfaction of the reader. When you have done this, and when your paper has been typed on computer in correct MLA format including an accurate Works Cited page, you are ready for a review of your paper by a peer.

PEER REVIEW: Have a fellow student read and evaluate the cause and effect argument.

_____ Make sure the final sentence of the introductory paragraph of a cause/effect paper clearly states a thesis in cause/effect structure. Example: "If the soccer players don't drink enough water, they will get dehydrated."

_____ List below the causes and their effects explored in this paper.

Causes	Effects
_____	_____
_____	_____
_____	_____
_____	_____
_____	_____
_____	_____
_____	_____
_____	_____
_____	_____

_____ Make sure the writer has used clear and
unambiguous language.

_____ Evaluate the structure and confirm that each
paragraph has only one central idea.

_____ Delete unnecessary details.

_____ Be sure all connections and transitions between
sentences and paragraphs are effective.

_____ Review the Works Cited page for accurate format
based on the *MLA Handbook*.

_____ List any relevant questions on the topic the author
has failed to answer.

PLANNING THE REWRITE

In addition to carefully considering the suggestions of the peer review, see also the helpful suggestions on page 46 of the *MLA Handbook* on "Writing Drafts." Rewrite the cause and effect paper into a smooth-flowing and logical discourse that clearly shows the links between the various causes and effects you have identified.

CHAPTER 10: DEDUCTIVE ARGUMENT

The linear logic of cause/effect reasoning discussed in the previous chapter is characteristic of the Christian and Western tradition and is often required by college writing teachers: If A is true, then B is true. The next step for thinkers trained in linear logic is the syllogism, which adds one or more components. Writers become like detectives who realize it can be *deduced* that if A is true, and if B is true, then C is true. Example: "If all freshmen take tests, and if Caleb is a freshman, then Caleb will take tests." This is a syllogism.

Arguments that can be reduced to syllogisms are sound arguments, and writers who argue based on a syllogism are less likely to fall into logical fallacies. The Apostle Paul wrote in Romans 10:9, "If you confess with your mouth, 'Jesus is Lord,' and believe in your heart that God raised him from the dead, you will be saved." This concise statement reduces the message of the entire New Testament to a syllogism that would make sense for a Roman audience trained in the type of logic based on linear thinking:

If A is true: <u>if you confess with your mouth, "Jesus is Lord"</u>

 And If B is true: <u>believe in your heart that God raised him from the dead</u>

Then C is true: <u>you will be saved</u>.

 In this argument both conditions have to be true before the conclusion is true—it is a *conjunctive* argument. By contrast, a *disjunctive* argument would read, "If A is true, **or** if B is true, then C is true. The beauty of a syllogism is that it reduces an argument to its essence—very useful when trying to identify the exact thesis of a written argument.

 The Apostle Paul's conjunctive syllogism targeted an audience that appreciated the linear logic taught by the Greek philosopher Socrates (469-399 BC), an early practitioner of logic admired by the Christian philosopher Augustin (AD 354-430), author of *City of God*:[16]

> Socrates … directed the entire effort of philosophy to the correction and regulation of manners, all who went before him having expended their greatest efforts in the investigation of physical, that is, natural

---

[16] This author is often spelled "Augustin<u>e</u>," but not in this source.

phenomena.... For he saw ... causes he believed to be ultimately reducible to nothing else than the will of the one true and supreme God,— [17]and on this account he thought they could only be comprehended by a purified mind; and therefore that all diligence ought to be given to the purification of the life by good morals, in order that the mind, delivered from the depressing weight of lusts, might raise itself upward by its native vigor to eternal things, and might, with purified understanding, contemplate that nature which is incorporeal and unchangeable light, where live the causes of all created natures. (145-146)

Plato (427-347 BC), a student of Socrates, is credited with combining the active and contemplative parts of philosophy and organizing it into three parts. Augustin identifies the three parts as "the first moral, which is chiefly occupied with action; the second natural, of which the object is contemplation; and the third rational, which discriminates between the true and the false" (146).

---

[17] A comma followed by a dash (,—) is not correct MLA style, but it is a faithful reproduction of the original and therefore must be retained in the quote.

Christian philosophers appreciate Plato because he said about God, "In Him are to be found the cause of existence, the ultimate reason for the understanding, and the end in reference to which the whole life is to be regulated. Of which three things, the first is understood to pertain to the natural, the second to the rational, and the third to the moral part of philosophy" (Augustin 147). This same view of God is presented in John 1:1-4:

Before time itself was measured, the Voice was speaking. The Voice was and is God. [2] This *celestial* Word remained ever present with the Creator; [3]His speech shaped the entire cosmos. *Immersed in the practice of creating,* all things that exist were birthed in Him. [4] His breath filled all things....

Aristotle (384-322 BC) studied under Plato for 20 years and later perfected the syllogism. A very basic introduction to Aristotelian logic appears below.

SYLLOGISMS SHAPE SOUND ARGUMENTS[18]

A logically *valid* syllogism is one in which the *reasoning* from premises to a conclusion is *accurate*:

All women are intelligent.

---

[18] Information in this section derives from Goodpaster 134-192.

Kendra is a woman.

Therefore, Kendra is intelligent.

This argument is logically valid because the *reasoning* is accurate. That is, if the major and minor premises are true (the first and second sentences), then the conclusion also must be true. However, since it is not true that all women are intelligent, the major premise is false and therefore the conclusion must be false. **Insight:** *A <u>valid</u> syllogism can yield a false conclusion.*

Also be aware that the conclusion of a *valid* syllogism with false premises could still be true, but not because of the premises:

All Irishmen are aggressive.

Ivan is an Irishman.

Therefore, Ivan is aggressive.

The structure of the above syllogism is *valid*, but the first premise is obviously false.

Similarly, it is possible to have a syllogism that is not valid—the *reasoning* is inaccurate—even though it has true premises and even a true conclusion:

Some animals are brown.

All dogs are animals.

Therefore, some dogs are brown.

Each premise is true, and the conclusion is true, yet the syllogism is invalid—the conclusion cannot reasonably be derived from the premises.

Confusing causes with effects often results in syllogisms that are true but not valid. To say that "all freshmen take tests," and that "Tonya takes tests," therefore "Tonya is a freshman" is not valid because other people besides just freshmen take tests. Reversing the order results in a syllogism that is both valid and true:

All freshmen take tests.

Tonya is a freshman.

Therefore, Tonya takes tests.

Insight: The *validity* of an argument depends on its form, not on the truth of its premises. Consequently, an argument that depends on false premises could be valid, and an argument based on true premises could be invalid. Only premises and conclusions are *true* or *false*.

A sound argument is both *valid* and *true*. The goal of linear logic is to develop syllogisms that have both true premises and valid reasoning—this results in a sound *deductive* argument. This is the form used by many church fathers to structure persuasive theological arguments and is still respected today. Writing students who can reduce their argument to a thesis statement in the form of a syllogism have taken the first step to writing convincingly and persuasively using linear logic that will impress teachers from cultures shaped by Aristotelian logic.

No matter whether a writer uses deductive argument described here or the inductive argument form discussed in the next chapter, it is vital to avoid errors in reasoning known as logical fallacies. Writers who commit logical fallacies destroy their own credibility and fail to persuade.

LOGICAL FALLACIES

A logical fallacy is an error in reasoning. Dr. Michael C. Labossiere has identified 42 such fallacies (see http://www.nizkor.org/features/fallacies/), and an internet search will turn up many different names for the same reasoning errors. A shorter list is provided here of the more common types:

A **hasty generalization** occurs when a writer draws a conclusion based on too little evidence: "Look at the damage those skateboarders are doing to the park bench. All those 'sidewalk surfers' are destructive." Write down a similar example common in your experience:

_____

_____

Similarly, the **stereotype** ascribes a common group trait to an individual: "He's a university student—he must be brilliant." Usually stereotypes are negative, as in, "Oh, he's from Subterranea, and all Subterraneans are lazy." Write down a similar example common in your experience:

_____

_____

An **appeal to the crowd** argument uses irrational fears and prejudices to persuade: "If we buy oil from Russia, those Communists will take over the world using our money!" Write down a similar example common in your experience:

_____

_____

A **non sequitur** (Latin for "it does not follow") draws unwarranted conclusions from irrelevant evidence: "Tony really chews through the groceries. He'll soon be seriously overweight." Write down a similar example common in your experience:

_____

_____

The **either/or** fallacy presumes that only two choices exist when actually there are many alternatives: "Unless we find a cure for AIDS, the human race will be wiped out." Write down a similar example common in your experience:

_____

_____

Begging the question, or "petitio principii" (Latin), refers to an issue in a formal debate that one side may ask the other side to concede in order to speed up the proceedings. But such a statement is illegitimate because it argues for the truth of an unproven statement: "Because the higher speed limit is responsible for so many deaths, it should be reduced." Write down a similar example common in your experience:

_____

_____

A **circular argument** uses repetition to replace proofs: "That painting is the most beautiful art in the room because it is better than the others." Write down a similar example common in your experience:

_____

_____

Arguing off the point ignores the question by introducing irrelevant material and redirecting the debate. This technique is routinely practiced by politicians. When asked, "What will you do to reduce crime in the neighborhood?" they are likely to say, "Our police force is underpaid and overworked, which is exasperated by the deterioration of the nuclear family, and the current administration is more concerned about what roads to pave than about how to make those very roads safe to drive down." Write down a similar example common in your experience:

_____

_____

The **ad hominem** (Latin for "to the man") argument attacks the individual rather than addressing the issue: "Professor Gibson doesn't deserve a promotion to the next faculty rank. He's always writing letters to the editor and he has a troubled marriage." This attack ignores the issue of whether Gibson deserves a promotion based on his job performance. Write down a similar example common in your experience:

_____

_____

The **faulty analogy** assumes that two things are similar when in fact they are not: "If America can land a person on the moon and bring him safely back to earth, certainly we can solve the problem of global warming." Write down a similar example common in your experience:

_____

_____

Post hoc, ergo propter hoc (Latin for "after this, therefore because of this") refers to an error in cause and effect reasoning (see previous chapter for discussion of cause and effect). Write down a similar example common in your experience:

_____

_____

Internet Assignment: Type "logical fallacy" in the space provided on your internet search engine and visit five websites that discuss these issues. Make a chart like the one illustrated below and summarize the most important thing you learn by visiting each of the five sites.

Website 1: _____

What I learned: _____

Website 2: _____

What I learned: _____

Website 3: _____

What I learned: _____

Website 4: _____

What I learned: _____

Website 5: _____

What I learned: _____

PRE-WRITING ASSIGNMENT

What is an important argument in your area of interest that particularly fascinates you? Just as the Apostle Paul faced the pressing issues of explaining the good news about Jesus to a skeptical audience, so you will find it necessary to argue convincingly for something vital in your academic field. Writing such an argument will draw on all the work you have done throughout this text, and will also require additional research. It is likely that your instructor will require an argument of at least eight pages of careful reasoning. Topic of interest:

_____

Vital issue within topic:

_____

Common questions about the issue:

1. _____

2. _____

3. _____

4. _____

5. _____

Possible answers to the questions:

1. _____

2. _____

3. _____

4. _____

5. _____

Now, make a syllogism out of the above information:

If A is true:

_____

and If B is true: _____

Then C is true: _____

The goal of *deductive* argument is often to achieve a "proof" that cannot be denied. By contrast, the goal of an *inductive* argument (the subject of the next chapter) is usually to provide compelling evidence that a given point of view is reasonable and plausible.

If you plan to write an argument using inductive reasoning, review the summary of the Scientific Method in Chapter 3 and the discussion of inductive argument in the next chapter. Next, make a list of the evidence you will need to collect, the sources of persuasive stories and information, and the steps you will need to follow in order to make your argument plausible and convincing.

DEDUCTIVE READING

Before exploring a sample deductive argument from the Bible, an important distinction must be made between the approach of theologians and literary critics. Leland Ryken notes that while biblical scholars tend to explore the text in a fragmented, line-by-line analysis that leans heavily on deductive reasoning, literary critics use more inductive reasoning by asking such questions as these: "How is the story structured? What are the unifying narrative principles? ... How does the story unfold sequentially? ...What are the plot conflicts, and how are they resolved? How does the protagonist develop as the story progresses? ... How is the thematic meaning of the story embodied in narrative form?" (28). Ryken notes that while literary criticism and biblical scholarship are complementary, they are vastly different and have different objectives.

Some authors such as the seventeenth-century writer John Bunyan used both methods. As a preacher he used linear logic as he expounded line by line, precept upon precept, on individual texts. But he also had the capacity, as Ryken describes it, to "respond with a child's sense of wonder to story, to sensations, to the weather, to elemental emotions such as terror or love or trust, to mystery, to miracle" (29).

Not all theologians bury themselves in the details. Inductive Bible study presents a way for theologians to read scripture as literature—far different from the systematic theology of a John Calvin, but natural to the informally educated like John Bunyan who tended to read scripture in a literal sense as *story*. The distinction is profound. Calvin's systematic theology leaned heavily on deductive argument in which the conclusion must be true if the premises are true. When the conclusion does not necessarily follow from the premises, a deductive argument is invalid. But the scriptures tell a story that is often more easily approached inductively by looking at what really happened as opposed to what should have happened based on the evidence. See Chapter 11 to explore the inductive approach in more detail.

Deductive Reasoning: Acts 6:8-7:60

[8] Stephen continually overflowed with extraordinary grace and power, and he was able to perform a number of miraculous signs and wonders in public view. [9] But

eventually a group arose to oppose Stephen *and the message to which his signs and wonders pointed.* (These men were from a group called the Free Synagogue and included Cyrenians, Alexandrians, Cilicians, and Asians.) [10] The Holy Spirit gave Stephen such wisdom in responding to their arguments that they were humiliated; [11] *in retaliation,* they spread a vicious rumor: "We heard Stephen speak blasphemies against Moses and God."

[12] Their rumor prompted an uprising that included common people, religious officials, and scholars. They surprised Stephen, grabbed him, and hauled him before the council. [13] They convinced some witnesses to give false testimony.

False Witnesses: This fellow constantly degrades the holy temple and mocks our holy law. [14] *With our own ears,* we've heard him say this Jesus fellow, this Nazarene *he's always talking about,* will actually destroy the holy temple and will try to change the sacred customs we received from Moses.

[15] The entire council turned its gaze on Stephen *to see how he would respond.* They *were shocked to* see his face radiant *with peace*—as if he were a heavenly messenger.

Acts 7

High Priest: *What do you have to say for yourself?* Are these accusations accurate?

Stephen: [2] Brothers, fathers, please listen to me. Our glorious God revealed Himself to our common ancestor Abraham, when he lived far away in Mesopotamia before he immigrated to Haran. [3] God gave him this command: "Leave your country. Leave your family *and your inheritance.* Move into unknown territory, where I will show you a new homeland." [4] First, he left Chaldea *in southern Mesopotamia* and settled in Haran until his father died. Then God led him still farther from his original home—until he settled here, in our land. [5] *But at that point,* God still hadn't given him any of this land as his permanent possession—not even the footprint under his sandal actually belonged to him yet. But God did give Abraham a promise—a promise that yes, someday, the entire land would indeed belong to him and his descendants. *Of course, this promise was all the more amazing because* at that moment, Abraham had no descendants at all.

[6] God said that Abraham's descendants would first live in a foreign country as resident aliens, *as refugees,* for 400 years. During this time, they would be enslaved and treated horribly. *But that would not be the end of the*

story. ⁷ God promised, "I will judge the nation that enslaves them," and "I will bring them to this mountain to serve Me." ⁸ God gave him the covenant ritual of circumcision *as a sign of His sacred promise*. When Abraham fathered his son, Isaac, he performed this ritual of circumcision on the eighth day. Then Isaac fathered Jacob, and Jacob fathered the twelve patriarchs.

⁹ The patriarchs were jealous of *their brother* Joseph, so they sold him as a slave into Egypt. Even so, God was with him; ¹⁰ and *time after time,* God rescued Joseph from whatever trials befell him. God gave Joseph the favor and wisdom *to overcome each adversity* and eventually to win the confidence and respect of *his captors, including* Pharaoh, the king of Egypt himself. So Pharaoh entrusted his whole nation and his whole household to Joseph's stewardship. ¹¹ *Some time later,* a terrible famine spread through the entire region—from Canaan down to Egypt—and everyone suffered greatly. Our ancestors, *living here in the region of Canaan,* could find nothing to eat. ¹² Jacob heard that Egypt had stores of grain; so he sent our forefathers, *his sons, to procure food* there. ¹³ Later, when they returned to Egypt a second time, Joseph revealed his true identity to them. He also told Pharaoh his family story.

¹⁴⁻¹⁶ Joseph then invited his father Jacob and all his clan to come and live with him in Egypt. So Jacob came, along with 75 extended family members. After their deaths, their remains were brought back to this land so they could be buried in the same tomb where Abraham *had buried Sarah* (he had purchased the tomb for a certain amount of silver from the family of Hamor in *the town of* Shechem).

¹⁷ Still God's promise to Abraham had not yet been fulfilled, but the time for that fulfillment was drawing very near. In the meantime, our ancestors living in Egypt rapidly multiplied. ¹⁸ Eventually a new king came to power—one who had not known Joseph *when he was the most powerful man in Egypt.* ¹⁹ This new leader *feared the growing population of our ancestors and* manipulated them for his own benefit, eventually seeking to control their population by forcing them to abandon their infants so they would die. ²⁰ Into this horrible situation *our ancestor* Moses was born, and he was a beautiful child in God's eyes. He was raised for three months in his father's home, ²¹ and then he was abandoned *as the brutal regime required.* However, Pharaoh's daughter found, adopted, and raised him as her own son. ²² So Moses learned the culture and wisdom of the Egyptians and became a powerful man—both as

an intellectual and as a leader. [23] When he reached the age of 40, his heart drew him to visit his kinfolk, our ancestors, the Israelites. [24] During his visit, he saw one of our people being wronged, and he took sides with our people by killing an Egyptian. [25] He thought his kinfolk would recognize him as their God-given liberator, but they didn't realize *who he was and what he represented.*

[26] The next day Moses was walking among the Israelites again when he observed a fight—but this time, it was between two Israelites. He intervened and tried to reconcile the men. "You two are brothers," he said. "Why do you attack each other?" [27] But the aggressor pushed Moses away and responded *with contempt*: "Who made you our prince and judge? [28] Are you going to slay me *and hide my body* as you did with the Egyptian yesterday?" [29] Realizing this murder had not gone unnoticed, he quickly escaped Egypt and lived as a refugee in the land of Midian. He *married there and* had two sons.

[30] Forty more years passed. One day while Moses was in the desert near Mount Sinai, a heavenly messenger appeared to him in the flames of a burning bush. [31] The phenomenon intrigued Moses; and as he approached for a closer look, he heard a voice—the voice of the Lord: [32] "I am the God of your own fathers,

the God of Abraham, Isaac, and Jacob." This terrified Moses—he began to tremble and looked away in fear. [33] The voice continued: "Take off your sandals *and stand barefoot on the ground in My presence*, for this ground is holy ground. [34] I have avidly watched how My people are being mistreated by the Egyptians. I have heard their groaning *at the treatment of their oppressors*. I am descending *personally* to rescue them. So get up. I'm sending you to Egypt."

[35] *Now remember:* this was the same Moses who had been rejected by his kinfolk when they said, "Who made you our prince and judge?" This man, *rejected by his own people,* was the one God had truly sent and commissioned by the heavenly messenger who appeared in the bush, to be their leader and deliverer.

[36] Moses indeed led our ancestors to freedom, and he performed miraculous signs and wonders in Egypt, at the Red Sea, and in the wilderness over a period of 40 years. [37] This Moses promised our ancestors, "The Eternal One your God will raise up from among your people a Prophet who will be like me." [38] This is the same one who led the people to Mount Sinai, where a heavenly messenger spoke to him and our ancestors, and who received the living message of God to give to us.

[39] But our ancestors still resisted. They again pushed Moses away and refused to follow him. In their hearts, they were ready to return to *their former slavery in Egypt.* [40] *While Moses was on the mountain communing with God,* they begged Aaron to make idols to lead them. "We have no idea what happened to this fellow, Moses, who brought us from Egypt," they said. [41] So they made a calf as their new god, and they even sacrificed to it and celebrated an object they had fabricated *as if it was their God.*

[42] *And you remember what God did next:* He let them go. He turned from them and let them follow their idolatrous path—worshiping sun, moon, and stars *just as their unenlightened neighbors did.* The prophet *Amos* spoke for God *about this horrible betrayal*: Did you offer Me sacrifices or give Me offerings during your 40-year wilderness journey, you Israelites? [43] *No, but* you have taken along your sacred tent for the worship of Moloch, and you honored the star of Rompha, your false god. So, if you want to worship your man-made images, you may do so—beyond Babylon.

[44] Now recall that our ancestors had a sacred tent in the wilderness, the tent God directed Moses to build according to the pattern revealed to him. [45] When Joshua led our ancestors to dispossess the nations God drove out

before them, our ancestors carried this sacred tent. It remained here in the land until the time of David.

[46] David found favor with God and asked Him for permission to build a permanent structure *(rather than a portable tent)* to honor Him. [47] It was, of course, Solomon who actually built God's house. [48] Yet we all know the Most High God doesn't actually dwell in structures made by human hands, as the prophet *Isaiah* said,

[49] "Since My throne is heaven

and since My footstool is earth—

What kind of structure can you build to contain Me?

What *man-made* space could provide Me a resting place?" asks the Eternal One.

[50]   "Didn't I make all things with My own hand?"

Stephen: [51] You stubborn, stiff-necked people! Sure, you are physically Jews, but you are no different from outsiders in your hearts and ears! You are just like your ancestors, constantly fighting against the Holy Spirit. [52] Didn't your ancestors persecute the prophets? First, they killed those prophets who predicted the coming of the Just One; and now, you have betrayed and murdered the Just One Himself! [53] Yes, you received the law as given by heavenly messengers, but you haven't kept the law which you received.

[54] Upon hearing this, *his audience could contain themselves no longer*. They boiled in fury at Stephen; they clenched their jaws and ground their teeth. [55] But Stephen was filled with the Holy Spirit. Gazing upward into heaven, he saw *something they couldn't see:* the glory of God, and Jesus standing at His right hand.

Stephen: [56] Look, I see the heavens opening! I see the Son of Man standing at the right hand of God!

[57] At this, they covered their ears and started shouting. The whole crowd rushed at Stephen, converged on him, [58] dragged him out of the city, and stoned him.

They laid their coats at the feet of a young man named Saul, [59] while they were pelting Stephen with rocks.

Stephen *(as rocks fell upon him)***:** Lord Jesus, receive my spirit.

[60] Then he knelt *in prayer*, shouting at the top of his lungs,

Stephen: Lord, do not hold this evil against them!

Those were his final words; then he fell asleep *in death*.

ANALYSIS QUESTIONS

1. Identify the deductions reached by Stephen's audience as a result of hearing his argument.

2. How do their deductions differ from those Stephen has reached?

3. Discuss how it is possible that two people hearing the same evidence can reach opposite conclusions.

4. Explore in writing the author's purpose in narrating the story of Stephen. What is he trying to teach his audience?

5. Showing action is important in many arguments. In your opinion, what is the most exciting action that takes place in this story? Why do you like it?

6. Identify the main conflict surrounding this argument. Be specific about the details.

7. How does conflict make the argument more interesting?

8. From what point of view is this argument presented? How would the argument feel differently if it were told from the point of view of the high priest?

9. Stephen's argument, a narrative within a narrative, is used in this story to reveal character. In what ways do you feel you know Stephen the human being as well as Stephen the servant of Jesus better because

you have "heard" him work his way methodically through an argument?

10. What argument techniques of Stephen's can you borrow to enhance the quality of the argument you will write?

SAMPLE ARGUMENT

Students often find this writing assignment the most difficult of all. Therefore, a sample of the kind of systematic thinking necessary in deductive reasoning is provided below. Charles White, Professor of Christian Thought and History at Spring Arbor University, is a graduate of Harvard College (BA) and Boston University (MA, Ph.D.). This essay is the condensed introduction to a much longer essay.

Dr. White argues, (A) if we are to love God with our minds, and (B) if we are to give an answer for the hope that is in us, and (C) if our actions depend on our beliefs, then (D) we need systematic theology. No doubt many students reading this text believe themselves to have no interest in systematic theology, a concept they may not understand, perhaps haven't read about before, and have no idea that it might be valuable to them personally.

The objective in reading this argument is to see whether these views change—to see whether the argument succeeds. And if it does, then the powers of persuasion are shown to be very useful indeed, and these same students might well feel motivated to master the art of deductive reasoning and writing.

The Puzzle of Systematic Theology

By Charles Edward White

How can Christians worship God the Father, God the Son, and God the Holy Spirit and still say there is only one God? How can Jesus be both man and God at the same time? How can God be all-powerful and all-wise and still let there be so much undeserved suffering in the world? What happens to the people who die without ever having a chance to have faith in Christ? Can true believers lose their salvation? Or as the title of a book for teenagers asks, "If God loves me, why can't I get my locker open?"

These questions are just a few of the infinite number of theological questions the Bible never answers directly. There are thousands of subjects, ranging from the composition of the Godhead to the perseverance of the saints, which people wonder about, but find no definitive word from God. Yet if we are to love the

242

Lord with our mind, as well as our heart, soul, and strength, we cannot ignore everything the Lord has not revealed. Further, if we are to give an answer for the hope that is in us, we need to make sure that our answer makes sense. In addition, if we are to be adult in our understanding, we must see the implications of what the Lord has told us. Only the very young need specific rules for every circumstance; with maturity comes the ability to apply general principles to various situations. Finally, because our actions often depend on our beliefs, those beliefs must be correct. Paul rebukes the Corinthians for letting a mistaken theology of the resurrection lead them into personal sin. Thus we all need systematic theology.

Systematic theology attempts to answer the questions God never addresses in the Bible. It aims to show how the various truths he has revealed relate to each other and to fill in the gaps between those revelations. It seeks to understand all the implications of what God has said and to fit everything he has revealed into a coherent pattern. Just as a scientist seeks to understand the world by discovering the laws that explain the various phenomena of nature, so the systematic theologian looks for the fundamental principles that underlie all that God has revealed in Scripture.

But natural laws are not part of nature: They are human inferences based on observed data. Like everything human, our understanding of natural laws can be improved. Ptolemy observed the night sky and announced the law that every heavenly body moves in a circle around the earth. Copernicus observed the sky more closely and modified the law by saying that the planets move in a circle around the sun. Later Newton made still more observations and developed the law of universal gravitation stating that every heavenly body attracts every other one. In our century Einstein showed that the laws Newton identified apply to everything we can see, and currently scientists are trying to formulate one law, a "unified field theory," that will describe the behavior of atoms as well as nebula. Human science is subject to constant improvement.

Similarly, systematic theology is not part of God's revelation: It is human reasoning based on God's truth. Like natural science, it can be improved. In the third century Sabellius based his theology on the Scriptures that teach God's unity. A century later Arius likewise firmly grasped half of the truth, emphasizing those verses that teach the subordination of the Son to the

Father. It was not until Nicea that the church developed a theology that affirms both these truths. On some questions the mind of the church is settled: The idea of the Trinity is the standard of orthodoxy. In other areas, however, the discussion still goes on. Christians are still struggling to reconcile the seemingly divergent teachings of the Bible and to formulate in one coherent pattern all the Scripture teaches.

The struggle to develop a unified field theory that will explain all the Bible's teaching is a little bit like putting an old jigsaw puzzle together. Almost everyone has an old jigsaw puzzle around the house, but it is usually not in top condition. Often a few pieces get lost and sometimes even the original box comes up missing. Deprived of the picture of the finished puzzle to guide them and lacking some of the original pieces, puzzle workers have to rely on the shapes and colors of the remaining pieces for clues to the pattern of the puzzle. With a thirty-piece puzzle designed for a toddler reconstructing the puzzle is an easy task, but with a thousand-piece monster it is almost impossible. Is it any wonder people have trouble fitting the 31,145 verses of the Bible into a systematic pattern?

People have trouble doing systematic theology because not all the pieces they want are there. The Bible clearly teaches that God is absolutely sovereign: That is one piece we must fit in. But the Bible just as clearly teaches that humans are free and responsible for their actions. That is another piece of the puzzle. Unfortunately for us, the pieces that connect God's sovereignty and human freedom are missing from the Bible. Given the pieces we have to work with, there is no way we can fit them together.

Besides not having all the pieces we want, a bigger problem with the puzzle of theology is that we do not have the box with the picture to show us what the finished puzzle looks like. Which pieces go in the center and which go on the edge? Do the pieces with one flat side make the border as one would expect or is this a very sophisticated puzzle with an irregular border and four flat matching quarters coming together in the middle?

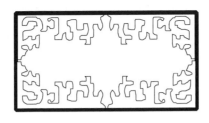

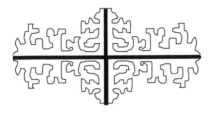

Faced with the problem of putting together an old jigsaw puzzle, people have to adopt certain rules. First, they must use every piece of the puzzle. They will never reconstruct the original if they simply throw away the pieces they find hard to fit. Second, they must not cut or modify any piece of the puzzle. Cutting off a knob from one piece is not the correct way to make it fit with another. Third, they are allowed to construct new pieces to fill in the gaps between the old pieces. This process is simply replacing what has been lost. Finally, the finished work must display a picture of something. After all, the challenge of a jigsaw puzzle is reconstructing the picture that has been taken apart.

247

The rules that apply to old jigsaw puzzles also apply to systematic theology. First, use every piece of the puzzle. We cannot simply ignore the Scripture's teaching about hell because we do not like it. All scripture is profitable for doctrine so we must not throw any of it away. Next, we must not cut the pieces we are given. The Jesus-pieces we find in Scripture contain more statements about God's judgment than about his love. We cannot trim away the harsh words to make the pieces fit into a portrait of Jesus meek and mild. We can, however, construct new pieces to make the original ones fit together. The doctrine of the Trinity is an obvious example. Though nowhere taught in Scripture, it holds together the Scripture's teaching of the unity and diversity in the Godhead. Our final job as systematic theologians is to construct a picture that makes sense. Some ideas are central, while others are peripheral. We must determine the organizing themes of Scripture and fit all the other ideas into their pattern.

Systematicians have the most disagreement in this area. Just as puzzle makers might disagree about whether they are putting together the picture of a horse or a dog, so theologians working on the soteriology section of the puzzle will disagree about what is central in the Bible's doctrine of our salvation. Although Calvin himself did not do so, some of his followers see the sovereignty of God as the central fact in human salvation. They speak much about God's power, his grace for the elect, and the efficacy of his decrees, but do not say much about how his actions are loving or just to the reprobate whom he elected for damnation before the foundation of the world. Thus when they assemble this section of the puzzle of theology, they see a huge throne in the center and little hearts out on the edge. Others argue that the central picture is really a cross, and that God's love and justice shape all the Bible's teaching about our salvation. For them God's sovereignty is present in the picture, but it is way out on the border of their thought.

It may be that someone will devise a way to put this section of the puzzle together that does equal justice to God's sovereignty, love, and justice. This formulation will eventually win the approbation of the whole church the way the thought of Athanasius enlightened the early Christians about the Trinity. We should be thankful that earlier thinkers have done so much of the work for us. When we approach the puzzle today we find that the first seven ecumenical councils put together some of the pieces to produce coherent pictures of the Godhead and of Christ. Our job is to put together the rest including the sections on pneumatology, soteriology, anthropology, and ecclesiology. Someday we may all agree on how it all fits together, but probably we will keep working on it until the puzzle maker himself returns and shows us where everything belongs.

ANALYSIS QUESTIONS

11. In what ways did the author's logical thinking process make it easier to follow the argument?

12. What did you learn about the assumptions behind systematic theology that you had not considered before?

13. Dr. White's essay is an argument by analogy. How effective was the analogy in helping you understand, accept, and appreciate his argument?

14. Which of Dr. White's argument methods will you consider using to make your own argument more persuasive?

WRITING ASSIGNMENT: OUTLINE

Review the notes you wrote in the pre-writing section of this chapter, then begin writing your own argument. Your topic should relate in some way to the papers you have previously written and should have a useful application to your major field of study in college.

Put the paper in standard MLA format including footnotes and a Works Cited page. The instructor will tell you the required length. When writing a deductive argument, it is vital to follow a deliberate logical structure. The format below is strongly recommended:

Introductory Paragraph: Use several introductory sentences to explain the issue, why it is important, and how it will be approached. Even if this is not a deductive argument, this paragraph should *contain the essence* of the syllogism developed earlier. If the argument *is* deductive, this thesis should be written *in the form* of a logical syllogism. This introduction can be up to half a page in length.

Supporting Argument One: Most arguments have a minimum of three supporting arguments, all of which have been outlined and summarized in the first paragraph. The first supporting argument can be from several paragraphs to several pages.

Supporting Argument Two: The second supporting argument and is likely to be of approximately the same length as the previous section.

Supporting Argument Three: This section contains the third supporting argument. Additional supporting arguments may be included as necessary.

<u>Conclusion</u>: The conclusion reviews, summarizes, and
clenches the argument presented in the preceding
pages.

ANALYZING AN ARGUMENT

Carry out your research by writing one literature
review for each source you select. As you transfer
information from your literature reviews into the
argument paper, be sure to avoid plagiarism by
accurately identifying sources, using parenthetical
references correctly, and including each source in the
Works Cited. Make sure to carefully follow all
formatting and punctuation guidelines provided in the
MLA Handbook.

As you study the various publications that will
serve as sources for your literature reviews, notice that
authors frequently make a case for some action or
interpretation of events by presenting claims backed by
reasons and evidence. Examine the logical soundness of
the author's case by evaluating the line of reasoning and
the use of evidence.

1. Ask what is claimed.

   a. Figure out what that claim assumes. Are the
   assumptions stated or unstated?

b. Ferret out the logical fallacies if you can identify any.

c. Discover what is offered as evidence, support, or proof.

d. Examine what is explicitly stated, claimed, or concluded.

e. Look for what is not stated but necessarily follows from what is stated.

2. Think of an alternative explanation and counter-examples.

3. Consider additional evidence that might weaken or strengthen the claims.

4. Determine what changes in the argument would make the reasoning more convincing.

5. Evaluate each source using the above guidelines. This will help you detect flawed arguments, select the best material, and develop your paper in a convincing way.

PEER REVIEW

Have a fellow student read and evaluate the argument paper, preferably someone who has also written an argument paper in the same format.

An argument usually expresses an assertion **(thesis)** about a **subject** to an **audience** for a particular reason

(purpose). Read the student argument and answer these questions:

1. Is the argument deductive or inductive? (See Chapter 11 about inductive arguments to understand the difference). If inductive, the thesis should summarize the scope of the investigation; if deductive, the thesis should resemble the form of a logical syllogism.

2. **Subject:** What is this essay about?

_____

_____

3. **Thesis:** What particular point is the author trying to make about this subject?

_____

_____

4. **Audience:** To whom is the author writing? How does its intended audience help shape the essay and influence its language and style?

_____

_____

5. **Purpose:** Why is the author writing this? To entertain? To inform? To persuade?

_____

_____

6. Evaluate the material based on the criteria outlined by Michael Osborn in Chapter 11. Both deductive and

inductive arguments have the potential to achieve these criteria:

A How effective is this material in the <u>elevation of the mind</u>?

_____

_____

B <u>Superior structure</u>: Evaluate the structure to determine how superior it is.

_____

_____

C <u>Bold imagery</u>: What imagery does the author use, and how bold is it?

_____

_____

D What <u>great challenge</u> does the writer place before his readers?

_____

_____

E To what extent do you experience <u>transport</u> from reading this? Why?

_____

_____

7. Aristotle presents three argument strategies: *Ethos* (ethical appeal), *Pathos* (emotional appeal), and *Logos* (rational appeal). Next to each paragraph,

identify which strategy is being used and how effective it is.

8. How successfully does this argument mix the writing strategies taught in previous chapters (narrative, description, process, definition, illustration, classification, comparison)? Try to identify places where one or more of these strategies could be used to strengthen the argument.

PLANNING THE REWRITE

A: Locate one of the most influential arguments in your field of study and write down the author, title, and other needed details for your Works Cited.

B: Evaluate that material based on the criteria outlined by Michael Osborn:

1. How effective is this material in the <u>elevation of the mind</u>?

2. <u>Superior structure</u>: Evaluate the structure to determine how superior it is.

3. <u>Bold imagery</u>: What imagery does the author use, and how bold is it?

4. What <u>great challenge</u> does the writer place before his readers?

5. To what extent do you experience <u>transport</u> from reading this? Why?

C. Give the main reasons why you think the argument identified above has influence in your field of study.

D: Evaluate the first draft of your own argument using the above criteria, then rewrite it based on your own critique as well as the input from your classmate's peer review.

CHAPTER 11: INDUCTIVE ARGUMENT

Inductive argument does not rely on the logical syllogisms and absolute proofs of deductive argument. Rather, it relies on accumulated evidence to infer strong probabilities. Example: "If the refrigerator is not running and the milk, butter, and cheese are spoiled, then the meat is probably rotten as well." There is no direct relationship between the dairy products and the meat. There is no precise cause and effect. There is just that uneasy feeling that things kept in refrigerators don't keep so well without *refrigeration.* There is also that horrible smell....

Inductive argument has both ancient and recent roots. Augustin writes that all the philosophers before Socrates "expended their greatest efforts in the investigation of physical, that is, natural phenomena" (145). This study of natural phenomena was revived two thousand years later when the English philosopher Francis Bacon (1561-1626) developed an experimental or inductive system of thinking known today as the

Scientific Method.[19] Bacon's *Novum Organum* (*New Instrument of Learning*) proposed replacing Aristotle's logic with inductive reasoning based on raw evidence found in nature.

Inductive reasoning results in plausible theories as opposed to proven facts. When proof is not possible, it is reasonable to adopt the more modest goal of proposing a conclusion that is *probably* true. If the same experiment is conducted 100 times and the results are always the same, the result will *probably* be the same on the 101st try—but there are no guarantees!

Much of the reasoning people do in everyday life is inductive—it produces *probable* conclusions rather than definite ones. Physicians accurately guess at the probable cause of a patient's symptoms without a definitive diagnosis. "I've seen 300 cases with these symptoms this month," they may say. "The prescription drug XYZ has cured everybody else—maybe it'll work for you...." Similarly, legal scholars frequently use inductive methods to determine what law governs a particular case, and journalists write editorials that lead to probable conclusions. All of them reach "reasonable"

---

[19] See Chapter 3, "The Scientific Method" for a summary of this system of organizing and conducting an experiment.

conclusions, and such reasoning pervades world cultures.

Inductive reasoning appeals to the creative side of the brain as opposed to the analytical side. Consider this example:

MONKEY HEART

Once upon a time, along a large river in Africa, there was a tree. In the tree lived a monkey. In the water beneath the tree a crocodile slept away the lazy days and dreamed about how delicious it would be to have a monkey sandwich. But he couldn't climb trees, so he thought hard about what to do. One day he said to the monkey, "We both have a friend on the other side of the river. He needs our help. How about if you and I go over there and help him?"

"But I can't swim across the river," said the monkey. "You will have to go alone."

"It is not suitable for me to go alone," he replied. "I will swim across the river and you can ride on my back."

Crocodiles are *good swimmers*, the monkey thought. Finally he said, "Okay, that is a good plan," and the monkey dropped down on the crocodile's back.

They started out, and when they got half way across the rushing water the crocodile said, "Oh! There is one thing I forgot to tell you."

"What is that?"

"Well, there is only one thing that can help our friend, and that is the heart of a monkey."

This news distressed the monkey. He looked back and saw it was a long way to the safety of his tree. He ran up and down, up and down the back of the crocodile, wondering what to do. Then, in a flash of inspiration, he ran to the head of the crocodile and spoke directly into its ear. "Oh dear," said the monkey. "We have a terrible problem!"

"And what might that be?" grinned the crocodile.

"I forgot to tell you—I have left my heart back there in my tree!"

"Is that so?" asked the surprised crocodile.

"Oh yes indeed! We monkeys never travel with our hearts. We must go back and get it."

The disappointed crocodile made a U-turn and swam under a low branch of the tree. The monkey leaped for the branch and scrambled up. Safely away, he called down to the crocodile, "I have found my heart, but I have also changed my mind. I think I'll just stay up here in my tree, where my heart is" (Bates 146-147).

The above inductive argument can be made into a syllogism:

If you guard your heart

And if you do not listen to lies

Then you will be safe.

However, such an argument may not be as compelling as the story itself. And there are cultural reasons to avoid stating a case using linear logic. Satoshi Ishii writes that in Japan it is considered rude to make a clear and direct point. The accepted practice is to delicately imply a conclusion after carefully approaching the issue from several angles. In Ishii's culture there is no equivalent to thesis statements and topic sentences (97-102). Unfortunately, many western teachers who do not recognize the structures of inductive arguments often assign poor grades to students from other cultures where inductive reasoning is the norm.

The structure of inductive logic may be envisioned in many ways. Duane Elmer describes typical African preaching as a daisy-shaped presentation in which the speaker continually loops back to a central point after each story, illustration, or scripture reading. The strength of the argument builds each time the speaker reiterates the central point. Elmer writes, "There is something amazingly effective about this speaking style…. I benefited more from this circular, flower petal style than from many of the linear sermons" (156). This pattern turns up in the "I Have a Dream" speech by Martin Luther King, Jr. that appears later in this chapter.

ANTHANASIUS THE GREAT

The inductive approach to argument can be traced back to St. Anthanasius the Great (AD 251-356), an Egyptian monk who established a monastery near Alexandria. His advice was prized, most famously by Constantine Augustus and his sons, Constantius Augustus and Constans Augustus.

Anthanasius advised the Greeks, "You lean on sophistical debates; and yet your monstrous idols are coming to naught, while our faith is spreading everywhere" (101). His disdain for deductive logic comes through when he quips, "You with your syllogisms and sophisms do not draw any [converts] from Christianity to Hellenism; we, teaching faith in Christ, despoil your superstition." Anthanasius then cast out the demons from some people standing there, "and the so-called philosophers were astonished and really stupefied at his wisdom and at the miracle that was done" (101-102).

Anthanasius taught that those who have faith in Christ "will no longer seek proofs by reasonings, but will think faith in Christ sufficient by itself" (104). He argues, "We win men by faith, which lays hold of real things before argument can logically establish them" (103). He reasons that knowledge about God must begin with faith: "Faith comes from the very build of the soul; but the art of logic from the skill of those who framed it. It follows that, to those who have an active belief, reasoned proofs are needless and probably useless. For what we know by faith, that you are trying to establish by argument. And often you cannot even put in words what we know; so that the action of faith is better and surer than your sophist's proofs" (101).

Anthanasius does not discredit the value of deductive logic in some circumstances. His point is that inductive reasoning has validity in matters of faith. The inductive approach provides a way to set aside personal prejudice and to see the Scriptures as God's story of his own active involvement in history. In essence, the inductive approach relies on what Beth Lynch calls "a willingness to 'experience' the text." She references Keats' concept of "negative capability" to experience uncertainty, mystery, and doubt without reaching after fact and reason (45). Asaph demonstrates this capacity in the passage below.

INDUCTIVE READINGS
Psalm 74

O True God, why have You *turned Your back on us and* abandoned us forever? Why is *Your anger seething and* Your wrath smoldering against the sheep of Your pasture?

[2] Remember the congregation *of people* You acquired long ago, the tribe which You redeemed to be Your very own. *Remember* Mount Zion, where You *have chosen to* live! [3] *Come,* direct Your attention to Your sanctuary; our enemy has demolished everything and left it in complete ruin.

[4] Your enemies roared *like lions* in Your sacred chamber; they have claimed it with their own standards as signs. [5] They acted like lumberjacks swinging their axes to cut down a stand of trees.

[6] They hacked up all the *beautifully* carved items, smashed them *to splinters* with their axes and hammers.

[7] They have burned Your sanctuary to the ground; they have desecrated the place where Your *holy* name lived in honor; [8] They have plotted in their hearts, "We will crush them and bring them to their knees!" Then they scorched

all of the places in the land where the True God met His people.

⁹ We no longer receive signs, there are no more prophets who remain, and not one of us knows how long *this situation will last*. ¹⁰ O True God, how much longer will the enemy mock us? Will this insult continue against You forever? ¹¹ Why do You stand by and do nothing? Unleash Your power and finish them off!

¹² Even so, the True God is my King from long ago, bringing salvation *to His people* throughout the land. ¹³ You have divided the sea with Your power; You shattered the skulls of the creatures of the sea; ¹⁴ You smashed the heads of Leviathan and fed his remains to the people of the desert.

¹⁵ You broke open *the earth* and springs burst forth and streams filled *the crevices*; You dried up the great rivers. ¹⁶ The day and the night are both Yours—You fashioned the sun, moon, *and all the lights that pierce the darkness*. ¹⁷ You have arranged the earth, set all its boundaries; You are the Architect of *the seasons*: summer and winter.

¹⁸ Eternal One, do not forget that the enemy has taunted You and a company of fools has rejected Your name. ¹⁹ We are Your *precious* turtledoves; don't surrender our souls to the wild beasts.

Do not forget the lives of Your poor, *afflicted, and brokenhearted ones* forever. [20] Be mindful of Your covenant *with us,* for the dark corners of the land are filled with pockets of violence. [21] Do not allow the persecuted to return without honor; may the poor, *wounded,* and needy sing praises *to You; may they bring glory* to Your name!

[22] O True God, rise up and defend Your cause; remember how the foolish man insults You every hour of the day. [23] Do not forget the voices of Your enemies, the commotion and chaos of Your foes, which continually grow.

ANALYSIS QUESTIONS

1. Why might a thinker focused only on deductive reasoning have difficulty understanding and explaining this text?
2. What does this author presume about the power of God in the first 11 verses?
3. Why do you think the writer feels he needs to remind God of his mighty works in verses 12-17?
4. In verses 18-23 the author presumes to tell the Almighty precisely how to run the world. How have the first 17 verses prepared the reader for the argument that concludes the passage?

5. One eternal philosophical question about God asks, "If God is all powerful, why is there evil in the world?" Another asks, "Why do the evil prosper while good people suffer?" In what ways does Asaph approach these issues? How successful is he?

6. What have you learned from this passage about inductive reasoning that will be useful in writing your own argument?

Jeremiah 12

Jeremiah: Eternal, You always do what is right when I bring a complaint Your way. So now let me put a case before You: Why do the wicked prosper so much? Why do all the untrustworthy have it so easy? [2]You plant them and watch them take root; You allow them to grow and even bear fruit. And yet, Your words mean nothing to them, deep down.

[3]Still, You know me, Eternal One; You see what is deep inside me. You've examined my heart, s*o why aren't they brought to justice?* Deal with them as sheep set aside for slaughter, singled out for death.

[4]How long must the land cry out in mourning, the grasses of the field wither *and bake in the sun*? The birds and wild animals have *simply* vanished, all because of

the wicked living here—because they say, "God does not see what will become of us."

⁵ **Eternal One:** If you are worn out after only running with *a few* men, how will you *one day* compete against horses? If you stumble on the easy terrain, how will you manage in the thick brush near the Jordan? ⁶*Jeremiah,* even your brothers and the rest of your family are ready to betray you. Even they cry out for your *death*; don't trust any of them, no matter how nicely they speak to your face.

⁷I have turned away My house, abandoned My heritage; I have given My deeply beloved one over to her enemies. ⁸My very own people have acted toward Me like a lion in the wild, roaring at Me *in defiance.* For this, I hate her.

⁹Have My own people become like colorful vultures? Are birds of prey circling all around them? Gather the wild beasts and bring them on to devour *My beloved.*

¹⁰Many shepherds have already destroyed My vineyard; they have crushed My fields. My beautiful land *of promise* has turned into a barren wasteland. ¹¹The very ground cries out to Me in this empty and forsaken land; the whole land is desolate, but no one seems to

care. [12]The destroyers pour over the bare hills in the desert as the sword of the Eternal devours the land from one end to another. There is no peace for anyone.

[13]The people planted wheat, but they will reap only thorns. *In the end,* there will be nothing to show for all their hard work. Shame will be their harvest because of the Eternal's burning anger *against them.*

[14] As for My wicked neighbors so eager to take away the inheritance I gave My people Israel, look! *There will come a day when* I will uproot them from their lands, and I will take Judah from their midst. [15] But after I have uprooted them *from their homelands,* I will have mercy on them and restore them to their own lands and their own possessions. [16]And if they diligently learn the ways of My people and *trust in Me instead of idols,* if they swear by My name saying, "As the Eternal lives," just as they taught My people to swear by Baal, then I will establish them alongside My people. [17] As for any nation that will not listen to *and follow My ways,* I will uproot it and destroy it completely. This is what the Eternal has declared.

ANALYSIS QUESTIONS

7. Paraphrase Jeremiah's complaint in verses 1-4 in your own words.

8. Paraphrase God's counter-complaint in verses 5-13 in your own words.

9. What about God's long-range perspective in verses 14-17 might comfort Jeremiah?

THE NATURE OF GREAT SPEAKING: I HAVE A DREAM

Michael Osborn argues convincingly that "I Have a Dream" is one of the greatest speeches in history. This claim challenges the notion that deductive logic is essential for successful argument. To assess whether his claims are true, first read King's speech, which follows.

I Have a Dream

I am happy to join with you today in what will go down in history as the greatest demonstration for freedom in the history of our nation.

[Part One] Five score years ago, a great American, in whose symbolic shadow we stand today, signed the Emancipation Proclamation. This momentous decree came as a great beacon light of hope to millions of Negro slaves who had been seared in the flames of withering injustice. It came as a joyous daybreak to end the long night of their captivity.

But one hundred years later, the Negro still is not free. One hundred years later, the life of the Negro is still sadly crippled by the manacles of segregation and the chains of discrimination. One hundred years later, the Negro lives on a lonely island of poverty in the midst of a vast ocean of material prosperity. One hundred years later, the Negro is still languishing in the corners of American society and finds himself an exile in his own land. So we have come here today to dramatize a shameful condition.

In a sense we have come to our nation's capital to cash a check. When the architects of our republic wrote the magnificent words of the Constitution and the Declaration of Independence, they were signing a promissory note to which every American was to fall heir. This note was a promise that all men, yes, black men as well as white men, would be guaranteed the unalienable rights of life, liberty, and the pursuit of happiness.

It is obvious today that America has defaulted on this promissory note insofar as her citizens of color are concerned. Instead of honoring this sacred obligation, America has given the Negro people a bad check, a check which has come back marked "insufficient funds." But we refuse to believe that the bank of justice is bankrupt. We refuse to believe that there are insufficient funds in the great vaults of opportunity of this nation. So we have come to cash this check—a check that will give us upon demand the riches of freedom and the security of justice. We have also come to this hallowed spot to remind America of the fierce urgency of now. This is no time to engage in the luxury of cooling off or to take the tranquilizing drug of gradualism. Now is the time to make real the promises of democracy. Now is the time to rise from the dark and desolate valley of segregation to the sunlit path of racial justice. Now is the time to lift our nation from the quick sands of racial injustice to the solid rock of brotherhood. Now is the time to make justice a reality for all of God's children.

[Part Two] It would be fatal for the nation to overlook the urgency of the moment. This sweltering summer of the Negro's legitimate discontent will not pass until there is an invigorating autumn of freedom and equality. Nineteen sixty-three is not an end, but a beginning. Those who hope that the Negro needed to blow off steam and will now be content will have a rude awakening if the nation returns to business as usual. There will be neither rest nor tranquility in America until the Negro is granted his citizenship rights. The whirlwinds of revolt will continue to shake the foundations of our nation until the bright day of justice emerges.

But there is something that I must say to my people who stand on the warm threshold which leads into the palace of justice. In the process of gaining our rightful place we must not be guilty of wrongful deeds. Let us not seek to satisfy our thirst for freedom by drinking from the cup of bitterness and hatred.

We must forever conduct our struggle on the high plane of dignity and discipline. We must not allow our creative protest to degenerate into physical violence. Again and again we must rise to the majestic heights of meeting physical force with soul force. The marvelous new militancy which has engulfed the Negro community must not lead us to a distrust of all white people, for many of our white brothers, as evidenced by their presence here today, have come to realize that their destiny is tied up with our destiny and their freedom is inextricably bound to our freedom. We cannot walk alone.

As we walk, we must make the pledge that we shall always march ahead. We cannot turn back. There are those who are asking the devotees of civil rights, "When will you be satisfied?" We can never be satisfied as long as the Negro is the victim of the unspeakable horrors of police brutality. We can never be satisfied, as long as our bodies, heavy with the fatigue of travel, cannot gain lodging in the motels of the highways and the hotels of the cities. We cannot be satisfied as long as the Negro's basic mobility is from a smaller ghetto to a larger one.We can never be satisfied as long as a Negro in Mississippi cannot vote and a Negro in New York believes he has nothing for which to vote. No, no, we are not satisfied, and we will not be satisfied until justice rolls down like waters and righteousness like a mighty stream.

I am not unmindful that some of you have come here out of great trials and tribulations. Some of you have come fresh from narrow jail cells. Some of you have come from areas where your quest for freedom left you battered by the storms of persecution and staggered by the winds of police brutality. You have been the veterans of creative suffering. Continue to work with the faith that unearned suffering is redemptive.

Go back to Mississippi, go back to Alabama, go back to South Carolina, go back to Georgia, go back to Louisiana, go back to the slums and ghettos of our northern cities, knowing that somehow this situation can and will be changed. Let us not wallow in the valley of despair.

[Part Three] I say to you today, my friends, that in spite of the difficulties and frustrations of the moment, I still have a dream. It is a dream deeply rooted in the American dream.

I have a dream that one day this nation will rise up and live out the true meaning of its creed: "We hold these truths to be self-evident: that all men are created equal."

I have a dream that one day on the red hills of Georgia the sons of former slaves and the sons of former slave owners will be able to sit down together at the table of brotherhood.

I have a dream that one day even the state of Mississippi, a state sweltering with the heat of injustice, sweltering with the heat of oppression, will be transformed into an oasis of freedom and justice.

I have a dream that my four little children will one day live in a nation where they will not be judged by the color of their skin but by the content of their character.

I have a dream today.

I have a dream that one day, down in Alabama, with its vicious racists, with its governor having his lips dripping with the words of interposition and nullification; one day right there in Alabama, little black boys and black girls will be able to join hands with little white boys and white girls as sisters and brothers.

I have a dream today.

I have a dream that one day every valley shall be exalted, every hill and mountain shall be made low, the rough places will be made plain, and the crooked places will be made straight, and the glory of the Lord shall be revealed, and all flesh shall see it together.

This is our hope. This is the faith that I go back to the South with. With this faith we will be able to hew out of the mountain of despair a stone of hope. With this faith we will be able to transform the jangling discords of our nation into a beautiful symphony of brotherhood. With this faith we will be able to work together, to pray together, to struggle together, to go to jail together, to stand up for freedom together, knowing that we will be free one day.

This will be the day when all of God's children will be able to sing with a new meaning, "My country, 'tis of thee, sweet land of liberty, of thee I sing. Land where my fathers died, land of the pilgrim's pride, from every mountainside, let freedom ring."

[Part Four] And if America is to be a great nation this must become true. So let freedom ring from the prodigious hilltops of New Hampshire. Let freedom ring from the mighty mountains of New York. Let freedom ring from the heightening Alleghenies of Pennsylvania!

Let freedom ring from the snowcapped Rockies of Colorado!

Let freedom ring from the curvaceous slopes of California!

But not only that; let freedom ring from Stone Mountain of Georgia!

Let freedom ring from Lookout Mountain of Tennessee!

Let freedom ring from every hill and molehill of Mississippi. From every mountainside, let freedom ring.

And when this happens, When we allow freedom to ring, when we let it ring from every village and every hamlet, from every state and every city, we will be able to speed up that day when all of God's children, black men and white men, Jews and Gentiles, Protestants and Catholics, will be able to join hands and sing in the words of the old Negro spiritual, "Free at last! free at last! thank God Almighty, we are free at last!"

WHY IT'S GREAT

Below are Michael Osborn's reasons for believing that "I Have a Dream" is one of the greatest speeches in history in its use of imagery. Two thousand years ago the Roman Longinus wrote *On the Sublime*, a study in great public speaking. "Sublimity is the echo of a great soul," says Longinus. Great speeches accomplish the following:

1. <u>Elevate the Mind</u>: If the speech is to be great, there must be greatness in the speaker. Aristotle observed that an audience will accept a speaker's message if the points are adequately proved. He said we have a divine spark in our nature that makes us receptive to greatness, and he captures this greatness with three words:

> *Ethos* (trust—enhanced by using reliable sources)
> *Pathos* (emotional appeal—good illustrations help)
> *Logos* (reason—logical delivery of argument)

When your critics are also won over, it is truly a great speech. King accomplishes this by calling on the constitution, associating himself with Lincoln and the Gettysburg address, and the hymn "Let Freedom Ring." By associating his movement with the vital symbols of American life, he put those who opposed him on the defensive and himself in the mainstream.

2. <u>Have Superior Structure</u>: The way material is organized, building to a dramatic climax, is vital. The broken American promise is spoken of in the shadow of the Lincoln Memorial. King uses four movements in the speech: 1. He expresses historical perspective and cultural outrage; 2. He exposes the nature of the

injustice—we can never be satisfied *until*.... This allows him to set up his agenda for social change; 3. He shares his dream—his vision of a better life. He moves from being an advocate to becoming a prophet who sees the future in all the fullness of its meaning; 4. He says, "Let freedom ring"—he wills his vision to be fulfilled and declares, "I've seen the promised land."

3. <u>Use Bold Imagery</u>: This passes the bounds of mere persuasion. With startling images we are drawn away from mere logic and brilliance. King makes us *see* his message. In his use of imagery, King is in the top five spokespersons in the history of western culture along with Demosthenes, finest of the ancient Greek world; Cicero, finest of the classical Roman orators; Edmond Burke, best of the British in the 18th century age of eloquence; and Abraham Lincoln, powerful American orator who used simple images with profound meanings.

4. <u>Present a Great Challenge</u>: Osborn adds to the Longinus criteria that some great cultural crisis must call forth greatness in the speaker to rise to the nobility of the moment.

What circumstance did King face?

_____

What circumstance do you face?

_____

No doubt that pressing concern will become the topic of your inductive argument.

5. Offer Transport: The effect of elevated language is not persuasion, but transport—sublimity flashing forth at the right moment … displaying the power of the orator in all of its fullness. It is almost like being born anew. The audience is given new eyes to see through. The meaning of their lives looks and feels different. King himself was forever different after this speech. He was transported into being a representative for freedom—he received the Nobel Peace Prize.

Osborn says great speeches offer depiction, emotion, and identification. They also incite to action, and they commemorate the past. Inductive argument is often superior to deductive argument for the same reasons. Longinus: "That is truly great which bears repeated examination, in which it is difficult or even impossible to withstand, and the memory of which is strong and hard to efface" (Osborn).

CHAPTER 12: INTEGRATION

The first section of this text taught the writing techniques of narrative, description, process, definition, illustration, and classification. The second section taught how to write comparison and media analysis essays. The third section taught the fundamentals of cause and effect, deductive, and inductive arguments. This final section invites students to write an integration paper by selecting material from all (or most) of the previous papers and combine them into one fully developed argument. Such integration requires three-dimensional writing that draws on all the writing styles taught in this text.

INTEGRATION READING

The book of Hebrews is a masterful integration paper drawing on more than 80 Old Testament passages to demonstrate in a powerful argument that the earlier covenant between God and humanity is fulfilled in Jesus Christ. The author uses all the knowledge of Jewish scripture and tradition as well as every tool of communication and persuasion available to him in this demonstration that both Hebrew and Gentile believers can and should be integrated into the one Church.

WRITING ASSIGNMENT

The first step is to establish an outline for the integration paper. This outline should be an expanded version of the structure recommended in the argument writing assignment from Chapter 10. Once the outline is established, it is relatively easy to cut and paste the material from previous papers into one document organized in such a way that it anticipates the reader's questions and answers them in a logical and satisfying manner. Once the basic structure is in place, the writer must tie the manuscript together with excellent transitions.

Transitions are words and phrases that serve as bridges from one paragraph to the next, one section to the next, and one chapter to the next. Transitions guide readers and prevent them from getting lost in the reading. Transitions serve as glue to hold an essay together.

Avoid over-using transitions. They are not needed between every sentence, but they are often needed between each paragraph. In a longer work, transition sentences and sometimes entire paragraphs are needed to guide the reader's thinking from what has been said so far to what will be explained next. Many kinds of transitions are possible, and a variety of examples are provided below.[20]

Transitions to emphasize a point

again / another key point / first thing to remember

for this reason / frequently / important to realize

indeed / in fact / to repeat

most compelling evidence

most important information

must be remembered

on the negative side / on the positive side

point often overlooked / significant that

surprisingly / truly / to emphasize

to point out / with this in mind

Transitions to show location

above / across / against / along / alongside

amid / Among around / away from / back of

behind / below / Beneath / beside / between

beyond / by / down / into / near / off

---

[20] Charts condensed from *Kim's Korner for Teacher Talk*.

on top of / outside / over / throughout / under

on / inside / in front of / in the center of

in the middle of / to the left / to the right

Transitions to compare items

as / also / accordingly / comparable to / like

likewise / similarly / sometimes / just as

in the same way / in conjunction with this

Transitions to contrast items

although / as opposed to / but / conversely

counter to / even so / even though / however

in spite of / in the meantime / otherwise

sometimes / still / yet / nevertheless

on the contrary / on the other hand

Transitions to show time

about / after / afterward / as soon as / at

at the same time / before / during / finally

first / later / in the meantime / meanwhile

last / next week / next time / next year

immediately / prior to / soon

yesterday / today / tomorrow

until / when / then / next

Transitions to clarify

for example / for instance / to illustrate

put another way / to clarify / simply stated

that is / stated differently

Transitions to add information

additionally / again / along with / also / and

another / as well / besides / equally important

finally / for example / for instance / further

furthermore / in addition / likewise / moreover

next / together with

Transitions to conclude or summarize

accordingly / as a result / consequently / due to

finally / in closing / in short / in summary

therefore thus / lastly / in the last analysis

logical conclusion is

Transitions to enumerate (to be used as sets)

first / second / third

first / next / last

one / also / in addition

one important / equally important / most important

in the beginning / toward the middle / at the end

a significant / another significant / of greatest
significance

HEART OF DARKNESS

In addition to words and phrases, writers also use
sentence and paragraph transitions to transition the
reader to the next phase of the presentation. A classic
example is provided by Joseph Conrad in *Heart of
Darkness* where for dozens of pages the reader has been
on a riverboat exploring the African interior. On the
return journey the narrator becomes extremely ill, and
the reader is efficiently transported back to civilization:

> No, they did not bury me, though there is a period
> of time which I remember mistily, with a shuddering
> wonder, like a passage through some inconceivable
> world that had no hope in it and no desire. <u>I found
> myself back in the sepulchral city</u> resenting the sight
> of people hurrying through the streets to filch a little
> money from each other, to devour their infamous
> cookery, to gulp their unwholesome beer, to dream
> their insignificant and silly dreams. (90)

In just eight words, "I found myself back in the
sepulchral city," Conrad transports the narrative to
another continent while showing the reader that darkness
is as pervasive in Europe as it is in Africa. Writers

employ this transition technique whenever cumbersome and unnecessary details get in the way.

LITERARY SCHEMES[21]

A final technique useful in writing a masterfully integrated argument is to deliberately use literary schemes to achieve a desired effect. Below is a list of the most easily recognized literary schemes and samples of each one:

1. Schemes of Construction

PARALLELISM: similarity of structure. **He ran for governor, he ran for congressman, and he ran for president.**

ANTITHESIS: juxtaposition of opposing ideas, often in parallel structure. **That's one small step for man, one giant leap for mankind.**

2. Schemes of Unusual or Inverted Word Order

ANASTROPHE: Inversion of the natural or usual word order. **Backward run the sentences.**

---

[21] See Corbett 45-59 for full discussion of these terms.

PARENTHESIS: insertion that interrupts the usual flow of the sentence. **He left work early (at least 3:30 seems early to me) to buy his wife a present.**

APPOSITION: placing side-by-side two co-ordinate elements, the second of which serves as an explanation or modification of the first. **Paula, my old boss, was at the party.**

3. Schemes of Omission

ELLIPSIS: deliberate omission of words that are implied. **He beat the world high jump record by four inches and the pole vault by six.**

ASYNDETON: deliberate omission of conjunctions. **I came, I saw, I conquered.**

POLYSYNDETON: deliberate use of many conjunctions. **The rain came down in sheets and the wind blew and the hail beat upon the rooftops.**

4. Schemes of Repetition

ALLITERATION/ASSONANCE: repetition of consonant/vowel sounds close together. **Already American vessels had been searched, seized, and sunk.**

ANAPHORA: repetition of the same word or group of words at the beginnings of successive clauses. **It is a** luxury, it is a privilege, it is an indulgence for those who are at their ease.

EPISTROPHE: repetition of the same word or group of words at the ends of successive clauses. **We cannot learn from one another until we stop shouting at one another.**

EPANALEPSIS: repetition at the end of a clause of the word that occurred at the beginning of the clause. **Blood hath bought blood, and blows have answered blows.**

ANADIPLOSIS: repetition of the last word of one clause at the beginning of the following clause. **He gave a confession, a confession that proved the court had executed the wrong man.**

CLIMAX: arrangement of words, phrases, or clauses in an order of increasing importance. **Let a man acknowledge obligations to his family, his country, and his God.**

ANTIMETABOLE: repetition of words, in successive clauses, in reverse grammatical order. **Mankind must put an end to war—or war will put an end to mankind.**

CHIASMUS: reversal of grammatical structures in successive phrases or clauses. **It is hard to make money, but to spend it is easy.**

POLYPTOTON: repetition of words derived from the same root. **Few are chosen because few choose to be chosen.**

ACTIVITY

See how many of the above literary schemes you can find in the following text:

Ecclesiastes 12

Teacher: *And so we come to the end of this musing over life. My advice to you is to* remember your Creator, *God,* while you are young: before life gets hard *and the injustice of old age comes upon you*—before the years arrive when pleasure feels far out of reach— [2] before the sun and light and the moon and stars fade to darkness and before cloud-covered skies return after the rain. [3] *Remember Him* before the *arms and legs of the* keeper of the house begin to tremble—before the strong *grow uneasy and* bent over *with age*—before toothless gums aren't able to chew food and eyes grow dim. [4] *Remember Him* before the doors are shut in the streets *and hearing fails* and everyday sounds fade away—before the *slightest* sound of a bird's chirp awakens the sleeping but the song itself has fallen silent. [5] People will be afraid of falling from heights and terrifying obstacles in the streets. *Realize that hair turns white* like the blossoms on the almond tree, one becomes slow *and large* like a *gluttonous* grasshopper, and *even caper berries* no longer stimulate desire. In the end, all must go to our eternal home while there are mourners in the streets. [6-7] So before the silver cord is snapped and the golden bowl is shattered: before the *earthen* jar is smashed at the spring and the wheel at the well is broken—before the dust returns to the earth that gave it and the spirit-breath returns to God who breathed it, let us remember our Creator. [8] Life is fleeting; *it just slips through your fingers.* All vanishes like mist.

[9] Not only did the teacher attain wisdom by careful observation, study, and setting out many proverbs, but he *was also generous* with his knowledge and *eagerly* shared it with people. [10] The teacher also searched for just the right words *to bring hope and encouragement,* and he wrote honestly about truth *and the realities of life.*

[11] The words of the wise are like goads; the collected sayings of the masters are like the nail-tipped sticks *used to drive the sheep,* given by one Shepherd.

[12] So be warned, my child, of anything else that might be said! There is no end to writing books, and excessive study only exhausts the body. [13] And, when all is said

and done, here is the last word: worship in reverence the one True God, and keep His commands, for this is *what God expects* of every person. [14] For God will judge every action—including everything done in secret—whether it be good or evil.

THE HONORS THESIS

The integration paper based on the content of all the assignments in this book is likely to grow into a long manuscript—possibly 25-40 pages. And if all the sources researched are included, the Works Cited may easily be two or three pages in length. Writing such a paper prepares students for the honors thesis that they may have the opportunity to write toward the end of their undergraduate program in college. At the very least, the integration paper will demonstrate the comprehensive knowledge gained throughout the semester, and reveal to the students that they have not only honed their writing and research skills, they have also attained a meaningful education within their chosen discipline and learned to effectively communicate what they know.

WORKS CITED

"Alexander Borodin: Biography." *Classic Cat.* Web. 17 Apr. 2009.

"Alexander Graham Bell: Inventor." *Lucid Café.* (29 Feb. 2008): n. pag. Web. 21 Apr. 2009.

Augustin. *City of God. Nicene and Post-Nicene Fathers,* vol. 2. Ed. Philip Schaff, 14 vols. Peabody, MA: Hendrickson, 2004. Print.

"APA Formatting and Style Guide." *The Owl at Perdue.* Web. 4 Apr. 2009.

Anthanasius the Great. *The Life of St. Anthony the Great.* Willits, CA: Eastern Orthodox Books, n.d. Date of original publication AD 357. Print.

Bach, Johann Sebastian. *Fugue in G Minor. Edition Bacakademie*. Dir. Helmuth Rilling, perf. Kay Johannsen, Organ Stiftschurch Grauhof. Holzgerlingen, Germany, 1999. CD.

Bates, Gerald E. "A Taste of African Imagination." *World Mission People: The Best of* The Missionary Tidings, *1990-95.* Ed. Daniel V. Runyon. Spring Arbor, MI: Saltbox Press, 1995: 146-147. Print.

The Bible. New International Version. Ed. Kenneth Barker. Grand Rapids: Zondervan, 2000. Print. Other editions cited in text where quoted.

Bulwer-Lytton, Edward George. *Pelham: Or The Adventures of a Gentleman*. Lincoln: U of Nebraska P, 1972. Print.

Bunyan, John. *The Holy War*. Ed. Daniel V. Runyon. Eugene, OR: Pickwick, 2012. Print.

Carr, Karen. "Socrates." *Kidipede—History for Kids*. Web. 17 Apr. 2009.

Chagomerana, Blessings. "Akafula for Short," *Tribal Bible: Stories of God from Oral Tradition*. Ed. Daniel V. Runyon. Spring Arbor, MI: Saltbox Press, 2014. Print.

Chesterton, G. K. "A Defence of Slang." *The Defendant*. London: J. M. Dent & Sons, 1901. Print.

Conrad, Joseph. *Heart of Darkness*. New York: Airmont, 1966. Print.

Corbett, Edward P. J. and Robert J. Connors. *Style and Statement*. New York: Oxford UP, 1998.

Dalton, Joan. "Applying Bloom's Taxonomy." *Good Questions are the Key to Good Research* (1986): n. pag. Web. 9 Apr. 2009.

Dartmouth Institute for Writing and Rhetoric. "Integrated Reading and Writing" (2013): n. pag. Web. 18 May 2014.

Dillard, Annie. *Teaching a Stone to Talk: Expeditions and Encounters.* New York: Harper & Row, 1982. Print.

Ellison, Ralph. *Invisible Man.* New York: Random House, 1980. Print.

Elmer, Duane. *Cross-Cultural Connections.* Downers Grove, IL: IVP Academic, 2002. Print.

Franklin, Benjamin. *The Abridged Autobiography of Benjamin Franklin*. Ed. Daniel V. Runyon. Spring Arbor, MI: Saltbox, 2014. Print.

Frye, Northrop. *Anatomy of Criticism.* Princeton: Princeton UP, 1957. Print.

---. *The Great Code: The Bible and Literature.* New York: Harcourt Brace Jovanovich, 1982. Print.

Gaebelein, Frank E., ed. *The Expositor's Bible Commentary.* 12 vols. Grand Rapids: Zondervan, 1976. Print.

Goodpaster, Jeffery R. *Thinking.* Upper Saddle River, NJ: Prentice Hall, 1999. Print.

Hemingway, Ernest. *For Whom the Bell Tolls.* New York: Charles Scribner's Sons, 1940. Print.

Henn, T. R. *The Bible as Literature.* New York: Oxford
UP, 1970. Print.

Ishii, Satoshi. "Thought Patterns as Modes of Rhetoric:
The United States and Japan." *Intercultural
Communication: A Reader.* Eds. Larry A. Samovar
and Richard E. Porter. 4th ed. Belmont, CA:
Wadsworth, 1985: 97-102. Print.

Jefferson, Thomas. Letter to Richard Price. 8 Jan. 1789.
The Thomas Jefferson Papers, Manuscript Division
of the Library of Congress. Web. 7 May 2009.

Kim's Korner for Teacher Talk. Ed. Kimberly Steele.
Web. 22 May 2009.

King, Jr., Martin Luther. "I Have a Dream." Lincoln
Memorial, Washington D.C. 28 Aug. 1963. Web.
25 May 2009.
<http://www.mlkonline.net/dream.html>.

Lewis, C. S. *Letters to Malcolm: Chiefly on Prayer.*
New York: Harcourt, Brace & World, 1964. Print.

---. *Miracles: A Preliminary Study.* New York:
Macmillan, 1948. Print.

---. *The Four Loves.* Oxford: Clarendon, 1967. Print.

Lincoln, Abraham. Second Inaugural Address. March 4,
1865. Yale Law School: The Avalon Project. 25
Oct. 2005. Web. 7 Apr. 2009.

Lynch, Beth. "'Rather Dark to Readers in General': Some Critical Casualties of John Bunyan's *Holy War* (1682)." *Bunyan Studies* 9 (1999/2000): 25-49. Print.

MLA Handbook for Writers of Research Papers: Seventh Edition. New York: The Modern Language Association of America, 2009. Print.

Newton, Isaac. "A Letter of Mr. Isaac Newton," *The Norton Anthology of English Literature*, 8th ed. Vol. 1. Ed. Stephen Greenblatt. New York: W. W. Norton, 2006: 2156-2160. Print.

Osborn, Michael. *I Have a Dream: The Nature of Great Speaking*. Davidson Films, n.d. Film.

Pushkin, Alexander. "The Queen of Spades." *Great Russian Short Stories*. New York: Bantam Doubleday Dell, 1958. Print.

Runyon, Daniel V. *The Shattered Urn: An Allegorical History of the Universe*. Spring Arbor, MI: Saltbox, 2014. Print.

Runyon, Kirby. Message to the author. 22 Sept. 2005. email.

Ryken, Leland. "Literary Criticism of the Bible: Some Fallacies." *Literary Interpretations of Biblical Narratives*. Ed. Kenneth R. R. Gros Louis. Nashville: Abingdon, 1974. Print.

---. *The Literature of the Bible.* Grand Rapids:
     Zondervan, 1974. Print.

"Sterile." *Shorter Oxford English Dictionary.* 5th ed.
     2002. Print.

Snyder, Howard A., with Daniel V. Runyon. *Decoding*
     the Church: Mapping the DNA of Christ's Body.
     Grand Rapids: Baker, 2002. Print.

Strunk, William, Jr., and E. B. White. *The Elements of*
     Style. Needham Heights, MA: Allen & Bacon,
     2000. Print.

Truss, Lynne. *Eats, Shoots & Leaves.* New York:
     Gotham Books, 2003. Print.

Twain, Mark. *The Innocents Abroad; or, The New*
     Pilgrims' Progress. Vol. 2. New York: Harper &
     Brothers, 1911. First published in 1869 by the
     American Publishing Company. Print.

---. "Continued Perplexities." *Life on the Mississippi.*
     London: Oxford UP, 1962. Print.

---. *Life on the Mississippi.* London: Oxford UP, 1973.
     Print.

Van Biema, David. "Why We Should Teach the Bible in
     Public School." *Time* 2 Apr. 2007: 40-46. Print.

Wellek, Rene and Austin Warren. "The Nature of
     Literature." *Theory of Literature.* 3rd ed. New
     York: Harcourt, Brace and World, 1956. Print.

White, Charles. "The Puzzle of Systematic Theology."
Unpublished essay, 2006. Print.

"The Wright Story." *First-to-Fly.* (28 Aug. 2006): n.
pag. Web. 17 Apr. 2009.